Testimonials

"Ethan Sawyer is an essay guru. His approach to essay work is insightful, inspirational, and fun. He helps students find their own unique voices and knows what colleges are looking for. Ethan is my number one choice for essay help."

—*Dr. Steven R. Antonoff, former dean of admission and financial aid, University of Denver, author of* College Match *and* College Finder

"Ethan teaches us the shape, the shift, the heft of the weapons, and the soft caresses that make words worth reading and remembering. His cinematic approach, his warm but literate and smart tone will help any student learn the beauty of shaping words into essays that work and play. This is one book applicants to college will want to read."

—*Parke Muth, consultant and former assistant dean of admission, University of Virginia*

"A must-have book for students and counselors! Sawyer's detailed steps make writing awesome college essays a breeze!"

—*Jennifer Kresock, independent counselor*

"Ethan's *College Essay Essentials* is the most concise and easy to follow 'how-to' guide out there... I cannot recommend Ethan and his approach more."

—*Rebekah Elmore, Peak College Consulting*

"With the gentle wisdom of a trusted shepherd, Ethan Sawyer brings the art of self-reflection and the craft of storytelling together brilliantly—and students respond with inspired, deep narratives worthy of respect by today's most discerning admissions officers. I can't imagine tackling an essay without it."

—*Jann Russell, College Fly*

"My advice to you if you are applying to college—get writing and get this book. Ethan will help guide them every step of the way until they have finished their college essays—ALL of them!"

—*Kelly Bates-Siegel, independent counselor*

"I've attended a lot of college essay classes, and read even more books on the subject, but nobody breaks it down quite so simply, yet elegantly, as Ethan. His essays and story examples are excellent and really highlight what college admissions departments are looking for. I highly recommend his new book!"

—*Gina Ney, college and career advisor*

"Yours was the best workshop I've attended in thirty years in the profession."

—*college counselor, on WACAC 2015 workshop session*

"If it weren't for your help and support, I don't think I would've gotten too 'personal' on my personal statement… Working with you was extremely helpful and rewarding… Thank you for loving what you do. Your love is now reflecting through us as we continue our journey."

—*Adriana S., student*

"By day two, [my daughter] was looking forward to going [to Ethan's class] and was so excited to see how her essay would develop by day's end. At the end of the three days, Dana's reaction was a sense of relief and excitement because she was completely done with her essay, she had crossed off a major task from her 'college to-do list,' and she was so very happy with how her essay turned out."

—*Erin C., parent*

College
Essay
ESSENTIALS

**A Step-by-Step Guide to Writing a
Successful College Admissions Essay**

Ethan Sawyer
College Essay Guy™

 sourcebooks

Published by Sourcebooks, Inc.
P.O. Box 4410, Naperville, Illinois 60567–4410
(630) 961-3900
Fax: (630) 961-2168
www.sourcebooks.com

Library of Congress Cataloging-in-Publication data is on file with the publisher.

Printed and bound in the United States of America.
VP 10 9

Contents

Why This Book

IMAGINE YOU'RE A SEVENTEEN-YEAR-OLD HIGH school senior given the task of writing a 650-word personal statement for your college application.

You're perplexed. Do you tell the story *of* your life or a story *from* your life? Do you choose a single moment? If so, which one? You feel your options are endless.

After an hour mulling over the possibilities, you're now more than perplexed—you're stressed. You start to wonder about what "they" (the admissions officers) want, even though you can neither predict nor have any control over their thoughts. So you start to panic. *What if they don't like what I write? What if I say the wrong thing? Is there a wrong thing?*

Then you remember you have just 650 words. That's one page of single-spaced Times New Roman to express the entire depth and complexity of who you are. You want to throw up.

Then you do.

★ ★ ★

This is the position many students find themselves in each year when it comes to writing the college application essay, an essay that—given the current landscape of college admissions—is arguably the most important 650 words a contemporary human will write.

But what if I told you, the seventeen-year-old high school senior, that your options aren't as endless as you might think? In fact, what if I told you that you only had *four* choices—just four potential paths you could take to write your essay?

And that, furthermore, you could choose a path by answering two simple questions.

Would that make things easier?

★ ★ ★

Tell me if this sounds like you:

a. You're worried about your essay because you don't know what you want to be when you grow up, or you don't have a sob story.

b. You do have a sob story, but you're worried it's too dramatic or that the reader will judge you for it.

c. You feel like you have too many options for stuff to write about, and you don't know how to pick.

d. You have a couple ideas, but you're not sure how to structure them.

e. You've written a draft, but you're not sure if it's any good.

f. You have some combination of all these, depending on the hour.

Here's the thing: no other college essay book out there helps you solve all these issues in an in-depth, step-by-step way.

But this book does.

QUESTIONS YOU MIGHT HAVE AND
WHERE YOU CAN FIND THE ANSWERS

How do I figure out what to write about?	page 1
How do I structure my essay?	page 13
Is there a step-by-step process for writing the essay?	page 39
Are any topics off-limits?	page 75
How much sharing is too much?	page 77
How do I revise my essay?	page 102
How do I make my essay not boring?	page 107
What are some different ways I can start my essay?	page 107
How do I show the reader I'm really smart?	page 112
How do I brag in a way that doesn't sound like I'm bragging?	page 119
How do I make my essay, like, deep?	page 121
How do I end my essay?	page 137
How do I know whether my essay is good or not?	page 183
I'm in a jam: How do I write my essay in one night?	page 202
Should I share my essay? With how many people? When?	page 204

That's right. This book answers all these questions.

And you don't even have to read the whole book.

You can jump around.

In a few minutes, you'll already be writing your essay. But first, let me tell you why I'm the perfect person to guide you through this process.

Why I'm the Perfect Person to Guide You through the Essay-Writing Process

THIS MAY SOUND WEIRD, BUT being the College Essay Guy is my dream job. Why? Not because, as a kid, I thought to myself, "I really want to be the College Essay Guy when I grow up." In fact, I first studied to become a screenwriter (BS in speech, Northwestern), then an actor (MFA, UC–Irvine), and then a counselor (Interchange Counseling Institute). And when I considered all the things that I loved to do and that I'd trained for—writing, speaking, counseling—I realized that I'd uniquely equipped myself to become the College Essay Guy. So I created this really cool job for myself.

How? To paraphrase Joseph Campbell, I followed my bliss. I kept doing what I loved until I found myself in this place.

But things really clicked for me when I realized how being the College Essay Guy actually brought together some of my core values, and I think sharing those with you here might help you understand why I'm the only person who could have written this book.

Here are some of my core values:

Practicality. I can't stand general writing advice that suggests,

"Use your authentic voice!" or "Write what you know!" Why? Because I have no idea what these things mean, and because they do not tell me *how* to do these things. I prefer advice that actually gets me from point A to point B.

Efficiency. I love getting things done and I especially love finding ways to streamline my productivity. (It's something I'm actually kind of obsessed with, and my wife likes to joke that in one day I can get done what it usually takes three people combined to finish.) It's why the word "essentials" is in the title of this book.

Vulnerability. I grew up as a missionary kid, moving twenty times before I graduated high school. Even though I often found myself meeting new people, I began to dislike small talk (either because I knew I'd be leaving soon anyway or because, well, small talk sucks), which is why when you meet me, I'll probably ask you some deeply personal question within the first five minutes. I'm interested in your deepest story. And I believe vulnerability is a more efficient way of finding that story.

So here's something that feels vulnerable for me to admit: the number one thing I look for when I meet people is their ability to listen and be present. If I sense someone is unwilling to at least try to listen and be present, I tend to distance myself emotionally for fear of being hurt. This feels vulnerable to admit because I think it makes me sound super judgmental. But I'm about to ask you to get vulnerable, so I figured I'd go first.

Patterns and connections. I loved watching movies as a kid, and those stories helped me make sense of my world. When I started teaching story structure to my college essay students, I loved how it helped them make sense of their worlds.

But it wasn't until I was introduced to narrative therapy that I really began to understand how powerful personal statement writing could be. Through narrative therapy, I discovered how I could reframe events of my past and, in effect, rewrite my identity. It was like learning a super-power. And guess what? You have this superpower, too. It's one you'll be upgrading as you read this book.

Insight. In college, one of my theater professors wrote the word "Illuminate!" at the bottom of a performance analysis I'd turned in. He was challenging me to answer "So what?" in a compelling way. I took his note to heart, and it's become something I strive for both in my work and in my life. It's something I challenge you to do, too.

Inspiration. I thrive on helping others realize their own brilliance, and I have worked to weave inspiration into every chapter of this book. In fact, if I had to sum up the goal of this book into one phrase, it would be this: I WANT TO INSPIRE YOU. And that feels extra vulnerable to share with you.

Which brings me to...

You. I believe in the person you are and in the person you are becoming. And that's what I believe your personal statement is—a record of your becoming.

So here's what you'll find in these pages: an efficient, practical process that will help you access your deepest story, recognize new patterns and connections, and generate insights that express how brilliant you are. Because you are.

But there's one more thing I haven't told you yet.

This process could change your life.

That's right. The personal statement writing process can be empowering, therapeutic, and even life-altering. Why? To paraphrase Joseph Campbell:

[A] good life is one hero journey after another.
Over and over again, you are called to the realm of adventure, you are called to new horizons.

Each time, there is the same problem: do I dare?
And then if you do dare, the dangers are there, and the help also, and the fulfillment or the fiasco.

There's always the possibility of a fiasco.

But there's also the possibility of bliss.

Writing your personal statement is a hero's journey. There are dangers. And there is the possibility that you might fail. But there's also the possibility that, if you stick with it, something amazing might happen.

Do you dare?

If so, continue to the next page.

How This Book Works

FIRST, YOU'LL SPEND ABOUT TWENTY minutes brainstorming.

Next, you'll spend ten minutes learning story structure and ten more minutes reading some sample essays and analysis.

Then I'll ask you two questions that point to four essay paths and you'll get to decide if you'd like to:

a. choose a path and start writing your essay, or
b. read about all four paths before choosing.

Then you'll write a draft of your essay.

Once your draft is done, I'll show you how to revise your essay, bring it to life, make it "like, deep," and then I'll introduce a few advanced essay-writing techniques.

Then you'll write a second draft (or third, or ninth) and come back to take The Great College Essay Test.

After that, I'll give you a few more step-by-step exercises to help you make sure your essay is doing what you want it to be doing, and finally you'll be ready for feedback (but do read my feedback tips first).

Quick note:

Even if you've already written a draft, I recommend reading the first four chapters anyway. It won't take long—I've designed the first part of the book so you can read it and write a draft in a day.

Sound good?

Let's do this.

CHAPTER ONE

Brainstorming

BEFORE WE DISCUSS *HOW* **TO** write the essay (structure), we need to know *what* we're writing about (content). I've used many brainstorming exercises over the years, but the following two are my favorites. They generate lots of ideas, and they get my heart pounding while I write.

ESSENCE OBJECTS EXERCISE

For this, you'll need a quiet place (or headphones) and about fifteen minutes.

Ready? Here we go:

- I want you to imagine a box.
- In this box is a set of objects.
- Imagine that each one of these is an "essence object" for you.
- What do I mean?
- Each object represents one of your fundamental qualities.
- So each object is more than just an object.

Example 1: My green pen. Why a green pen? I always carry a green pen because, like my mentor Cliff Faulkner, I grade nearly all my students' essays in green. Why green? Because red carries so many negative connotations—bad, wrong, warning—and when a student gets an essay back and it's covered in red marks, it can tend to look bloody, like a battlefield. But if a student gets an essay back that's covered in green, it looks verdant. Also, red means "stop" (like a stoplight), but green says "keep going." And that's the essence I want to communicate to my students: keep going. So my green pen is more than just a green pen.

Example 2: A well-worn North Carolina Tar Heels basketball. Why? I came home from the hospital wearing Carolina Blue, so I've been a Carolina fan, literally, since birth. I've spent more time on a basketball court than almost anywhere else (which is why the ball is well worn), and basketball represents my connection with my dad: when I was a kid, we'd watch Carolina games and play basketball for hours. In fact, basketball was one important way my dad showed he loved me. So this basketball is more than just a basketball.

Example 3: The blue Bible my grandma gave me when I was seven. This represents my having been raised in the Presbyterian Church. It represents Wednesday night potluck dinners, summer camp adventures, and trips with my youth group. So this Bible is more than just a Bible.

You get the idea.

I want you to make a list of twenty essence objects. (Don't complain—you're infinitely complex and creative and could come up with a thousand—I'm asking for only twenty.)

Note: No need to write what the objects mean to you as I've just done if you don't want to. You can just do this:

- green Precise V5 extra-fine rolling-ball pen
- worn-down North Carolina basketball

- blue Bible with my name stitched on it in gold lettering
- BBQ sauce
- annotated copy of *The Brothers Karamazov*
- friendship bracelet
- black-and-white composition notebook
- *Amélie* DVD
- Evanston Hockey T-shirt

If it helps, put on some music. Let your mind wander.
Begin now.

MY ESSENCE OBJECTS

Use your imagination.

(If you get stuck, you'll find questions on the next page to inspire you.)

THE BIG LIST OF BRAINSTORMING QUESTIONS

- ❒ What's a food that reminds you of your grandmother?
- ❒ What's an object that reminds you of home?
- ❒ An object that represents your father?
- ❒ Or, if you don't have a relationship with your father, what object reminds you of that absence in your life?
- ❒ What about your mother?
- ❒ What's something that makes you feel safe?
- ❒ What's something you lost?
- ❒ Something you forgot?
- ❒ What—or who—makes you laugh?
- ❒ Best book ever?
- ❒ What would your desert island movie be—the one you'd watch again and again?
- ❒ What piece of art consistently blows your mind?
- ❒ What object represents something you regret— something you wish you'd done differently?
- ❒ What's a secret you have? (Don't worry, this stays here.)
- ❒ What's something about you that no one else knows?

- ❒ Something you stole?
- ❒ Something you found?
- ❒ Something that makes you feel safe?
- ❒ What do you wish you were better at being or doing?
- ❒ The worst thing that ever happened to you?
- ❒ The last time you cried so hard that your breath caught in that halting way that it does when little kids cry? What mattered to you so much that it brought forth your deepest sobs?
- ❒ What's a challenge you faced?
- ❒ When you think about that challenge, what brought you through—what resources did you develop to overcome that difficulty?
- ❒ What would the logo on your imaginary business card be?
- ❒ What image would you have carved into your tombstone?
- ❒ An object that represents: a smell you love, a smell you hate, a taste you love, a taste you hate, the sweetest sound in the world?

☐ What's the coolest thing about science?

☐ Something that reminds you of being a kid?

☐ Something that represents a dream you have?

☐ What object represents your best friend? Your grandmother?

☐ When did you know? (Yes, that's the whole question.)

☐ What object represents a quality you have that you love but that people don't often recognize?

☐ What object represents the best advice you ever received?

☐ What's the best money you ever spent?

☐ What's your favorite word?

☐ Something you'll never get rid of?

☐ A bad habit?

☐ A perfect moment?

☐ A time you laughed so hard you cried?

☐ A time you cried so hard you laughed?

☐ An image you'll never forget?

☐ What would they put in the museum of your life?

☐ The cover image on your first self-titled album?

☐ An object representing a near-death experience?

☐ When did you feel most alive?

☐ What does a perfect Saturday night look like to you?

☐ A perfect Sunday afternoon?

☐ Best game ever—real or made up?

☐ Your favorite metaphor for life?

☐ When were you so embarrassed you wanted to disappear?

☐ What's a recurring dream you have?

☐ Your worst (actual) nightmare?

☐ When were you most afraid?

☐ If you had a clone, what would you have the clone do?

☐ When's a time you were speechless?

☐ The moment you left childhood behind?

☐ A quotation you love?

☐ Your favorite photo?

☐ A word that you love from another language?

☐ The biggest decision you've ever made?

Now survey your list and ask: Which essences or qualities are missing? What else could I include?

Write down two to three more essence objects.

(Google "100 Brave and Interesting Questions" for more.)

WHAT'S YOUR STORY?

FINDING THE RIGHT CLAY

Think of essay writing as sculpting. You're working to sculpt an essay that reflects something true about who you are. The purpose of the Essence Objects Exercise is to help you find the right clay. How can you be absolutely sure you're sculpting with the right clay? You can't. Writing is an art, after all, not a science. But here's a tip:

Tell your deepest story.

I was part of a story circle once in which we were asked to tell our deepest story. How can you tell when you've found yours? You'll feel it in your gut. It'll feel vulnerable (more on this on page 189). If you read it aloud and the writing sounds superficial or like it could have been written by any number of people, it's probably not your deepest story. So:

What's your deepest story?

Before moving on, spend three minutes jotting down answers to these questions:

What's the toughest lesson you've ever had to learn?

What was the hardest thing you've ever had to overcome?

What's your actual superpower? When did you learn you had it? How'd you develop it?

I wouldn't be who I am today without _____ _____.

If you have a specific career/major in mind, answer: Why am I a [writer/doctor/teacher]?

Do any of these answers connect to any of your essence objects?

CORE VALUES EXERCISE

Here's my other favorite brainstorming exercise, and it'll help you figure out the second half of your essay in about five minutes. To begin, pick your Top Ten values from the following list.

What do I value?

- community
- inspiration
- serenity
- physical challenge
- responsibility
- competition
- career
- practicality
- working with others
- freedom
- security
- strength
- self-control
- hunger
- personal development
- respect
- mindfulness
- culture
- bravery
- communication
- change and variety
- compassion
- nature

- intuition
- trust
- social justice
- intellect
- self-reliance
- financial gain
- laughter
- faith
- involvement
- adventure
- vulnerability
- adaptability
- restraint
- healthy boundaries
- friendship
- excellence
- meaning
- power
- privacy
- self-expression
- stability
- diversity
- love
- control
- surprise

- nutrition
- competence
- risk
- balance
- self-discipline
- courage
- family
- empathy
- working alone
- fun
- humility
- efficiency
- intensity
- health and fitness
- meaningful work
- my country
- music
- truth
- resourcefulness
- awareness
- art
- autonomy
- wit
- patience
- listening
- commitment

- ❐ leadership
- ❐ helping others
- ❐ meditation
- ❐ practicality
- ❐ creativity
- ❐ excitement
- ❐ collaboration
- ❐ social change
- ❐ beauty
- ❐ passion
- ❐ integrity
- ❐ ecological awareness
- ❐ quality relationships

- ❐ travel
- ❐ logic
- ❐ curiosity
- ❐ spirituality
- ❐ directness
- ❐ honesty
- ❐ independence
- ❐ multiplicity
- ❐ supervising others
- ❐ cooperation
- ❐ affection
- ❐ wisdom
- ❐ knowledge

- ❐ growth
- ❐ mystery
- ❐ order
- ❐ innovation
- ❐ accountability
- ❐ democracy
- ❐ religion
- ❐ experience
- ❐ _____
- ❐ _____
- ❐ _____
- ❐ _____
- ❐ _____

Now pick your Top Five.

- ❐ _____
- ❐ _____
- ❐ _____
- ❐ _____
- ❐ _____

Once you have those, pick your Top Three.

- ❐ _____
- ❐ _____
- ❐ _____

And then, yes, pick your Number One value. Remember that you're not losing any of the others, you're just picking the most important value for you <u>today</u>.

- ❐ _____

Don't read ahead until you've done this.

Really.

Finally, if you know what career you'd like to pursue—engineering, for example—put the first letter of that career ("E") beside five values of a great engineer. Maybe you write an "E" next to collaboration, autonomy, innovation, and helping others, and for a fifth value, you write "working with my hands" in one of the blanks at the end of the list.

Once that's done, set these aside. I'll tell you what to do with them in a little bit.

HOW THE ESSENCE OBJECTS AND CORE VALUES EXERCISES CAN HELP YOU WRITE YOUR ESSAY (AND YOUR LIFE)

That's right. You're not just writing your essay. You're writing your life. I'll explain in a second. First, let's talk about:

How These Exercises Can Help You Write Your Essay

T. S. Eliot once wrote: "The only way of expressing emotion in the form of art is by finding an 'objective correlative.'"

What's an objective correlative? It's an object to which you correlate emotions, memories, and complex meanings. It's an object that's more than an object.

Every object in your essence object box is an objective correlative for some important, complex part of you.

Think of each one as a hyperlink to your soul. Click on any one of those essence objects and there's a story behind it. At this point we don't know how many will end up in your story—one, fifteen, or none—but the essences they represent most certainly will be the college essay you submit.

I love the Core Values Exercise for a few reasons:

1. If we sat down and I asked you why your top value is your top value, I'd probably learn something pretty great about you.
2. I believe your values can serve as a magic glue for your essay, helping to connect your past with your present and future (more on this in a bit).
3. It can also help generate material for my favorite prompt:

Describe the world you come from and tell us how your world has shaped your dreams and aspirations.

Why is this my favorite prompt? Because I believe that if a student answers this question—and answers it well—then this essay can work for most personal statement prompts and even some scholarship essays. Working on this particular question can also lead to a lot of personal growth. And how could you apply the material from the Essence Objects and Core Values exercises to this prompt?

Like this:

Your essence objects = your world
Your core values = your dreams and aspirations

I'll explain this in more detail in chapter four, but your essence objects will help you generate content for the first half of your essay (your past) and your core values will help you map out the second half (your present and your future).

How the Core Values Exercise Can Help You Write Your Life

Let me emphasize something: the process of writing your personal statement is more than just reporting on the facts of your life—you're actually assigning them meaning in the larger context of your life. As one of my students told me recently as she was finishing her essays, "I feel like this process has helped me realize the importance of everything I've experienced."

And check it out: this process can help you understand not only your past, but also your future. Here's how:

Some people think of their career as the end goal, their answer to the question, "What are your dreams and aspirations?" But I believe that thinking is flawed.

Why? I believe your career (doctor, lawyer, sports trainer, and so on) isn't actually your end goal. Instead, I think your career is the means by which you will experience and express your values. In other words:

Your values *are* your dreams and aspirations.

An example from my life: my goal in life is not to be the College Essay Guy, but to help people connect more deeply with themselves, realize that it's okay to be vulnerable, and tell the stories of their lives in ways that can be useful and empowering. The College Essay Guy just happens to be my current platform, the way I'm manifesting these values in the world right now.

That's why it's so important to begin identifying your core values. Understanding your core values can give you some criteria for judging what your priorities are and what it might take for you to find happiness—both in work and in life.

So if you skipped the Core Values Exercise on page 8, go back and do it!

The question to consider when writing your essay is: Should you focus on a single overarching value or a wide variety of your core values? Should you focus on a single essence object or several? That depends on which structure you choose.

CHAPTER TWO

Structure

NARRATIVE VS. MONTAGE STRUCTURE

A Quick Screenwriting Lesson

Ever seen a movie that didn't make sense at all? Probably not, as those films tend to not get made. But have you ever tried telling a friend about a movie you watched and wondered why it didn't sound right? Chances are it had something to do with the structure of your retelling.

What's structure? Simply put, it's how you organize and emphasize all the story moments or events (i.e., all the stuff you want to say) in your essay. And I believe there are just two ways.

Why just two? Because I believe you must choose whether you want to organize your story:

a. using cause and effect (where one moment leads to the next), in which case you'll use **narrative structure**, or

b. thematically (where all the moments relate under a common idea), in which case you'll use **montage structure**.

Are there other structures? Perhaps, but I believe every story that connects events must connect them in a way that is either causal or not causal, so any other structure would be a variation on either narrative or montage structure.

Can you combine narrative and montage structures? Yes, but now we're getting ahead of ourselves—let's first learn how each one works.

Narrative Structure

Let's unpack the structure that most American films use. Learning this may change the way you watch films (it did for me). It's a structure as old as time, one that storytellers have been using for centuries. Joseph Campbell, an American writer and mythologist, called it the monomyth, or Hero's Journey. I'll refer to it as narrative structure. Its basic elements are:

1. Status quo
2. Inciting incident/Status quo change
3. Raise the stakes
4. Turning point/Moment of truth
5. Denouement/The final act
6. Outcome/New status quo

STATUS QUO

The main character in the story (hint: in your essay, that's you) is living his or her normal life. Often, there is a Main Problem the Main Character Must Solve.

INCITING INCIDENT/STATUS QUO CHANGE

One day, something happens. A boy discovers he is a wizard (*Harry Potter*). A girl falls down a rabbit hole (*Alice in Wonderland*). A murder happens (almost every mystery ever). Or: The Worst Thing That Could Happen to the Main Character...happens. You get the idea. In short, the hero is called to adventure.

RAISE THE STAKES

Things get more dangerous and important.

- In small dramas, the events become more important inwardly—in our main characters' personal lives—and the events of the story gradually build until they threaten to change their lives forever.
- In action movies, events become more important outwardly, escalating until not only our main characters are threatened, but also the country, the world, or (in big budget films) civilization as we know it.
- In some films, the main characters' inward journey (what they must learn) and outward journey (what they must do) are intertwined. See: *Star Wars*, *Inside Out*, *Avatar*.

TURNING POINT/MOMENT OF TRUTH

Often this is the climax—the moment of highest tension. The character must make the Ultimate Choice or Fight the Ultimate Battle.

- Will Beauty kiss the Beast and save his life? (*Beauty and the Beast*)
- Will Neo realize—and accept—his role as The One before it's too late? (*The Matrix*)
- Will Frodo destroy the Ring and save Middle Earth? (*Lord of the Rings*)

Sometimes it's the character deciding, "I've got to do something about this" or, "I'm mad as heck and I'm not going to take it anymore."

DENOUEMENT/THE FINAL ACT

What does the hero or heroine (again, in your essay, that's you) do about it? Fight, run, apologize, start a movement, or something else?

OUTCOME/NEW STATUS QUO

The result. Note that this should be different from the original status quo.

Montage Structure

WHAT IS A MONTAGE?

Montage is a technique that involves creating a new whole from separate fragments (pictures, words, music). In filmmaking, a montage is used to condense space and time so that information can be delivered in a more efficient way.

Take the classic "falling in love" montage that's commonly used in romantic comedies. We don't see every single moment or interaction between the couple as their relationship grows; instead, we see: she surprises him at work with a card she made, they walk through the park, they dance in the rain, they move boxes into their new home. You get the idea—a few images tell the whole story. And you can use this technique for your essay.

But which moments from your life should you choose? That's something we won't decide right this second—it'll take some time—but it's what will ultimately provide the building blocks for your essay. And remember that there's no right answer to that question, since essay writing is an art, not a science.

FIND A FOCUSING LENS

Montage essays employ what I call a focusing lens. You can't discuss every single aspect of your life, but you can show us a few important elements through a single lens, or metaphor.

What type of focusing lens might you use to write your essay? A sport? A place? An art form? A hobby?

Tips for Finding a Good Focusing Lens

1. Make it visual. Storytelling is a visual medium. Use a lens that

will help conjure images in the reader's mind. And, by the way, I don't recommend writing "soundtrack" or "mixtape" essays in which your favorite songs provide the soundtrack for your life, as the reader can't hear the music (and often doesn't know or have the same emotional connection as you do to the songs referenced). Be a painter—conjure some images in our mind.

2. Consider using something you know a lot about. Know how to cook? Use food. Play chess? Use that! Use your essence objects list for ideas.

3. Find a focusing lens that allows you to "go wide." Use a metaphor that will allow you to discuss several different aspects of who you are.

For more narrative structure essay examples and analyses, see pages 22, 26, 54, 56, 85, 87, and 173.

For more montage structure essay examples and analyses, see pages 24, 28, 65, 96, 99, and 211.

NARRATIVE VS. MONTAGE
STRUCTURE TAKEAWAYS

To make sure the difference between narrative and montage structures is really clear:

With Narrative Structure...

Think of the events being linked through cause and effect. For example:

I used to be really shy.

My shyness was really frustrating.

I knew I had to do something, so I tried a few different things. I failed at all of them.

Finally, I joined the debate club. At first it didn't go well.

But eventually I fell in love with it.

I started to come out of my shell and began improving in other areas of my life.

I'm no longer the shy kid—now I speak up and stand up for my beliefs.

This experience has led me to want to major in international relations and pursue a career in foreign diplomacy.

See how <u>one thing leads to another</u>, and how all the events are linked through cause and effect? That's what I'm calling narrative structure.

With Montage Structure...

Think of the events in a montage being linked <u>thematically</u>. For example:

My first lesson in behavioral economics came from my grandfather.

An experience with my dad taught me my second lesson in behavioral economics.

But it wasn't until I read *Freakonomics* that I began to actively examine the world through the lens of a behavioral economist.

Behavioral economics has provided me with an avenue to explore some of life's most complex questions.

Although there are no concrete answers to these questions, finding my passion for the social sciences has not only led me to a potential career path, but has also brought me closer to my family.

See how they're connected by a common theme? That <u>theme</u> is behavioral economics.

Remember that the key difference between narrative and montage structures is this:

- Narrative structure connects events <u>causally</u> (not "casually," but through cause and effect).
- Montage structure connects events <u>thematically</u>.

One final, important difference:

- With narrative structure, events are often chronological (they're mentioned in the order that they happened).
- With montage structure, there is more freedom to jump around in time.

Which structure should you choose?

That depends on the type of essay you're writing.

Unsure which type you want to write? Read on.

CHAPTER THREE

The Four Types of College Essays

I LOVE TO BEGIN MY private sessions and live workshops with these two questions:

1. Have you experienced challenges in your life?
2. Do you know what you want to be in the future?

So imagine I'm there right now, looking at you over a cup of tea, and I've just asked you these two questions.

Why these two questions? Because they point to four essay paths, and each path requires a different approach.

And before you choose a path, you must answer the questions.

No, really. This is an interactive book, so play along.

In fact, circle one:

1. Have you experienced significant challenges in your life?

    Yes   No

2. Do you know what you want to be in the future?

    Yes   No

Okay, the answers to these two questions break into four essay types:

A	B
Student **has** faced significant challenges and **does know** what he or she wants to study.	Student **has not** faced significant challenges and **does know** what he or she wants to study.
C	D
Student **has** faced significant challenges and **does not know** what he or she wants to study.	Student **has not** faced significant challenges and **does not know** what he or she wants to study.

Tip: Narrative structure tends to work well for essay types A and C, while montage structure tends to work well for types B and D. I'll say more in the upcoming step-by-step instructions, but I just wanted to plant this idea here.

Must you write about challenges in your essay if you have experienced them? No.

Must you write about your career if you know what it is? No.

You can write a great essay if you have or haven't experienced challenges and if you do or don't know what you want to study. Writing about challenges, however, can yield interesting material, and writing about a future career can help you shape your essay ending.

But you don't have to write about either. (I know I'm repeating myself, but I really want you to get that.)

In a moment I'll ask you to pick a type and dive in to the step-by-step guide for that type, but first let's look at an example of each one.

TYPE A: "WITH DEBATE"

Written by a student who did *face significant challenges and* did know *what she wanted to study*

The clock was remarkably slow as I sat, legs tightly crossed, squirming at my desk. "Just raise your hand," my mind pleaded, "ask." But despite my urgent need to visit the restroom, I remained seated, begging time to move faster. You see, I was that type of kid to eat French Fries dry because I couldn't confront the McDonalds cashier for some Heinz packets. I was also the type to sit crying in front of school instead of asking the office if it could check on my late ride. Essentially, I chose to struggle through a problem if the solution involved speaking out against it.

My diffidence was frustrating. My parents relied on me, the only one able to speak English, to guide them, and always anticipated the best from me. However, as calls for help grew, the more defunct I became. I felt that every move I made, it was a gamble between success and failure. For me, the fear of failure and disappointment far outweighed the possibility of triumph, so I took no action and chose to silently suffer under pressure.

Near meltdown, I knew something needed to be done. Mustering up the little courage I had, I sought ways to break out of my shell—without luck. Recreational art classes ended in three boring months. I gave up Self Defense after embarrassing myself in class. After-school band, library volunteering, and book clubs ended similarly. Continued effort yielded nothing.

Disillusioned and wrung dry of ideas, I followed my mom's advice and joined a debate club. As expected, the club only reaffirmed my self-doubt. Eye contact? Greater volume? No thanks.

But soon, the club moved on from "how to make a speech" lessons to the exploration of argumentation. We were taught to speak the language of Persuasion, and play the game of Debate. Eventually, I fell in love with it all.

By high school, I joined the school debate team, began socializing, and was even elected to head several clubs. I developed critical and analytical thinking skills, and learned how to think and speak spontaneously.

I became proud and confident. Moreover, I became eager to play my role in the family, and family relations strengthened. In fact, nowadays, my parents are interested in my school's newest gossip.

Four years with debate, and now I'm the kid up at the white board; the kid leading discussions; and the kid standing up for her beliefs.

More importantly, I now confront issues instead of avoiding them. It is exciting to discover solutions to problems that affect others, as I was able to do as part of the 1st Place team for the 2010 United Nations Global Debates Program on climate change and poverty. I take a natural interest in global issues, and plan to become a foreign affairs analyst or diplomat by studying international affairs with a focus on national identity.

In particular, I am interested in the North-South Korean tension. What irreconcilable differences have prompted a civilization to separate? Policy implications remain vague, and sovereignty theories have their limits—how do we determine what compromises are to be made? And on a personal level, why did my grandfather have to flee from his destroyed North Korean hometown—and why does it matter?

I see a reflection of myself in the divide at the 38th parallel because I see one part isolating itself in defense to outside threats, and another part coming out to face the world as one of the fastest-developing nations. Just as my shy persona before debate and extroverted character after debate are both part of who I am, the Korean civilization is also one. And just as my parents expect much from me, the first of my family to attend college, I have grand expectations for this field of study.

TYPE B: "ENDODONTICS"

Written by a student who did not *face significant challenges and* did know *what he wanted to study*

As a kid I was always curious. I was unafraid to ask questions and didn't worry how dumb they would make me sound. In second grade I enrolled in a summer science program and built a solar-powered oven that baked real cookies. I remember obsessing over the smallest details: Should I paint the oven black to absorb more heat? What about its shape? A spherical shape would allow for more volume, but would it trap heat as well as conventional rectangular ovens? Even then I was obsessed with the details of design.

And it didn't stop in second grade.

A few years later I designed my first pair of shoes, working for hours to perfect each detail, including whether the laces should be mineral white or diamond white. Even then I sensed that minor differences in tonality could make a huge impact and that different colors could evoke different responses.

In high school I moved on to more advanced projects, teaching myself how to take apart, repair, and customize cell phones. Whether I was adjusting the flex cords that connect the IPS LCD to the iPhone motherboard, or replacing the vibrator motor, I loved discovering the many engineering feats Apple overcame in its efforts to combine form with function.

And once I obtained my driver's license, I began working on cars. Many nights you'll find me in the garage replacing standard chrome trim with an elegant piano black finish or changing the threads on the stitching of the seats to add a personal touch, as I believe a few small changes can transform a generic product into a personalized work of art.

My love of details applies to my schoolwork too.

I'm the math geek who marvels at the fundamental theorems of Calculus, or who sees beauty in $A = (s(s - a)(s - b)(s - c))^{\wedge}(1 / 2)$. Again, it's in the details: one bracket off or one digit missing and the whole equation collapses. And details are more than details, they can mean the difference between negative and positive infinity, an impossible range of solutions.

I also love sharing this appreciation with others and have taken it upon myself to personally eradicate mathonumophobiconfundosis, my Calculus teacher's term for "extreme fear of Math." A small group of other students and I have devoted our after-school time to tutoring our peers in everything from Pre-Algebra to AP Calculus B/C and I believe my fluency in Hebrew and Farsi has helped me connect with some of my school's Israeli and Iranian students. There's nothing better than seeing a student solve a difficult problem without me saying anything.

You probably think I want to be a designer. Or perhaps an engineer?

Wrong. Well, kind of.

Actually, I want to study Endodontics, which is (I'll save you the Wikipedia look-up) a branch of dentistry that deals with the tooth pulp and the tissues surrounding the root of a tooth. As an Endodontist, I'll be working to repair damaged teeth by performing precision root canals and implementing dental crowns. Sound exciting? It is to me.

The fact is, it's not unlike the work I've been doing repairing cellphone circuits and modifying cars, though there is one small difference. In the future I'll still be working to repair machines, but this machine is one of the most sophisticated machines ever created: the human body. Here, my obsession with details will be as crucial as ever. A one millimeter difference can mean the difference between a successful root canal and a lawsuit.

The question is: Will the toothbrushes I hand out be mineral white or diamond white?

TYPE C: "RAISING ANTHONY"

Written by a student who did *face significant challenges and* did not know *what she wanted to study*

At age three, I was separated from my mother. The court gave full custody of both my baby brother and me to my father. Of course, at my young age, I had no clue what was going on. However, it did not take me long to realize that life with my father would not be without its difficulties.

My brother, Anthony, was eleven months old when my father placed us in the hands of our first babysitter. I remember being confused at first, wondering where my father had gone and when he would be back, but after a while, I became accustomed to this routine of absence and the never ending babysitters that filled in for him. These strangers consisted of college students, chain-smokers, senile women, and foreigners—all were technically adults, but not one was a suitable substitute for a parent. When my father was home, he still seemed absent; he was distant both physically and emotionally. He was busy bouncing from one girlfriend to the next, sleeping in until 1:30 in the afternoon, and sitting on the couch watching television. He took us out to restaurants every night and wasted the money he earned on expensive dinners, his current girlfriend, and liquor. This continued for ten years.

Legally, we had all the necessities to survive, but in truth our home was devoid of structure. Schoolwork went unchecked. Bedtimes were unregulated. Dust accumulated in thick layers on the paperwork that overflowed on the dining table. Often times, Anthony and I would spend hours waiting at school for someone to pick us up, and most of our dinners were served well past eleven at night.

Consequentially, and quite unwittingly, I shed my childhood and assumed the role of "parent" for Anthony before my seventh birthday. I memorized the routes we took to school and led Anthony home myself. I watched professional chefs on PBS and learned how to cook basic meals for two. Unfortunately, as I progressively developed into the parent, Anthony took advantage of our lack of true authority and grew into the epitome of a problem child. He became unruly, and his behavior soon bled into his school life. His grades suffered and he seemed to act out more often. His rash temper continued to grow until one day the school called our home because he had tried to throw a chair at his teacher.

Anthony was the only kindergartner in our school's history to be suspended. The school counselor recommended that when my father was in town we attend therapy as a family. But that accomplished nothing—my father's initial attempts to implement authority devolved quickly into apathy, and then he was traveling again. I, on the other hand, would not give up so easily. I became the watchful eye and mentor that Anthony and I both needed. I soaked in the parenting videos that our family counselor had given my dad. I explained to Anthony why a structured lifestyle is important and why retribution is needed for one's misdeeds. To further instill self-discipline in him, I would have him formulate his own penalties. I also began to follow up on his schoolwork by contacting his teachers. On one particularly hopeful afternoon I even tried to introduce him to books that I had read— but I learned I can't win every battle. I wasn't satisfied with just giving a fish to my little brother; I wanted to teach him how to cast lines himself and learn the tools of self-reliance. Looking back at my hectic childhood, I am grateful for the insight it afforded me, and I am grateful for the effect my little brother had on me.

Inadvertently, by raising Anthony I ended up raising myself. Living with my unreliable father and reliant younger brother gave me the need and incentive to find myself and to mature quickly. At a very early age I became resourceful, independent, and responsible. It makes me proud to know that I single-handedly raised Anthony and myself. I now know that I can face any challenge with confidence. Even if I don't succeed, I know I will be stronger just for trying.

TYPE D: "SCRAPBOOK"

Written by a student who did not face significant challenges and did not know what she wanted to study

I look at the ticking, white clock: it's eleven at night, my prime-time. I clear the carpet of the Sony camera charger, the faded Levi's, and last week's Statistics homework. Having prepared my workspace, I pull out two 12 by 12 crème sheets and reproduce sketches of the layouts already imprinted in my head. Now I can really begin.

I leave a quarter inch border as I cut the first photograph, which I then adhere to a polka-dotted paper. For a sophisticated touch, I use needle and thread to sew the papers together. Loads of snipping and pasting later, the clock reads three in the morning. I glance down at the final product and feel an overwhelming sense of pride as I brush my fingers over the many layers and pages. For me, the act of taking pieces of my life and putting them together on a page is my way of organizing remnants of my past to make something whole and complete. This particular project is the most valuable one to date: the scrapbook of my life.

In the center of the first page are the words MY WORLD

in periwinkle letters. All four of my Korean grandparents sit in the top corner, looking over my first birthday—my ddol. Underneath them are my cousins trying not to let go of their overwhelming laughter while playing "red light, green light" at O'Melveney Park. Meanwhile, my Texas relatives watch Daniel, the youngest, throw autumn leaves into the air that someone had spent hours raking up. To the right, my friends miserably pose for our history teacher who documents our droopy faces the morning of our first AP exam. The largest photograph is that of my family huddled in front of the fireplace, drinking my brother's hot cocoa and listening to the pitter-patter of sporadic Los Angeles rain.

I move over to the right side of the page. At the top, I have delicately sewn on three items. The first is a page of a Bible that was given to the soldiers at a Cambodian base where I taught English. Beneath is the picture of my group of Guatemalan girls devouring *arroz con pollo*, red sauce slobbered all over our lips. I reread the third item, a short note that a student of mine from a rural Korean school had struggled to write in her broken English. Moving down the page, I see the shelf display of my vibrantly glazed ceramic projects. I have included a clipping of my page from the school newspaper, next to ticket stubs for Wicked from my date with Dad. I made sure to incorporate a snapshot of my first scrapbook page featuring a visit to Hearst Castle on my tenth birthday.

After proudly looking over each detail, I turn to the next page, which I've labeled: AND BEYOND. This page is not cluttered or crowded. There is my college diploma with International Relations listed and the school's name left blank. A map covers nearly half the paper with stickers pinpointing locations all over the world, but I cannot recognize the countries' names. The remainder of the page is a series of frames with captions under-neath. Without the photographs, the descriptions are cryptic.

For now, that second page remains incomplete because I have no precise itinerary for my future. The red flags on the map represent the places I will travel to, possibly to teach English or to partner with a charity again. As for the empty frames, they will be filled with the people I will meet: a family of my own and the families I desire to help, through a career I have yet to adopt. Until these things unfold, all I can do is prepare. I'll continue to finalize the layout and gather materials so that I can start piecing together the next part, the next page of my life's scrapbook.

WHAT MAKES THESE ESSAYS GREAT: A BRIEF STRUCTURAL ANALYSIS

TYPE A: "WITH DEBATE"

Written by a student who did *face significant challenges and* did know *what she wanted to study*

Remember that narrative structure works well when relating challenges.

The clock was remarkably slow as I sat, legs tightly crossed, squirming at my desk. "Just raise your hand," my mind pleaded, "ask." But despite my urgent need to visit the restroom, I remained seated, begging time to move faster. You see, I was that type of kid to eat French Fries dry because I couldn't confront the McDonalds cashier for some Heinz packets. I was also the type to sit crying in front of school instead of asking the office if it could check on my late ride. Essentially, I chose to struggle through a problem if the solution involved speaking out against it.

Raise the stakes: it's important that she overcomes this problem not just for herself, but for her family.

Status quo (a.k.a. the main problem she must solve): she's really, really shy.

My diffidence was frustrating. My parents relied on me, the only one able to speak English, to guide them, and always anticipated the best from me. However, as calls for help grew, the more defunct I became.

I felt that every move I made, it was a gamble between success and failure. For me, the fear of failure and disappointment far outweighed the possibility of triumph, so I took no action and chose to silently suffer under pressure.

Near meltdown, I knew something needed to be done. Mustering up the little courage I had, I sought ways to break out of my shell—without luck. Recreational art classes ended in three boring months. I gave up Self Defense after embarrassing myself in class. After-school band, library volunteering, and book clubs ended similarly. Continued effort yielded nothing. Disillusioned and wrung dry of ideas, I followed my mom's advice and joined a debate club. As expected, the club only reaffirmed my self-doubt. Eye contact? Greater volume? No thanks.

But soon, the club moved on from "how to make a speech" lessons to the exploration of argumentation. We were taught to speak the language of Persuasion, and play the game of Debate. Eventually, I fell in love with it all.

By high school, I joined the school debate team, began socializing, and was even elected to head several clubs. I developed critical and analytical thinking skills, and learned how to think and speak spontaneously.

I became proud and confident. Moreover, I became eager to play my role in the family, and family relations strengthened. In fact, nowadays, my parents are interested in my school's newest gossip.

Four years with debate, and now I'm the kid up at the white board; the kid leading discussions; and the kid standing up for her beliefs.

More importantly, I now confront issues instead of avoiding them. It is exciting to discover solutions to problems that affect others, as I was able to do as part of the 1st Place team for the 2010 United Nations Global Debates Program on climate

Margin notes:

Raise the stakes even more: nothing is helping!

Inciting incident (a.k.a. the worst thing that could happen): Because what really shy kid would want to join the debate club?

Side note: Look how many core values she gets into these thirty-four words. (I count at least five.)

New status quo: though she was once too shy to ask for ketchup packets, look at her NOW.

Here she answers "so what" (see page 119 for how to brag in a subtle way).

change and poverty. I take a natural interest in global issues, and plan to become a foreign affairs analyst or diplomat by studying international affairs with a focus on national identity.

In particular, I am interested in the North-South Korean tension. What irreconcilable differences have prompted a civilization to separate? Policy implications remain vague, and sovereignty theories have their limits—how do we determine what compromises are to be made? And on a personal level, why did my grandfather have to flee from his destroyed North Korean hometown—and why does it matter?

Beautiful metaphor

I see a reflection of myself in the divide at the 38th parallel because I see one part isolating itself in defense to outside threats, and another part coming out to face the world as one of the fastest-developing nations. Just as my shy persona before debate and extroverted character after debate are both part of who I am, the Korean civilization is also one. And just as my parents expect much from me, the first of my family to attend college, I have grand expectations for this field of study.

and wonderful insight to close.

Oh, and by the way.

Remember that montage structure works well for this type of essay.

TYPE B: "ENDODONTICS"

Written by a student who did not face significant challenges and did know what he wanted to study

In this montage essay, the author describes a variety of values, all of which connect under the lens of endodontics.

As a kid I was always curious. I was unafraid to ask questions and didn't worry how dumb they would make me sound. In second grade I enrolled in a summer science program and built a solar-powered oven that baked real cookies. I remember obsessing over the smallest details: Should I paint the oven black to absorb more heat? What about its shape? A spherical shape would allow for more volume, but would it trap heat as well as conventional rectangular ovens? Even then I was obsessed with the details of design.

Core values: curiosity and meticulousness.

And it didn't stop in second grade.

A few years later I designed my first pair of shoes, working for hours to perfect each detail, including whether the laces should be mineral white or diamond white. Even then I sensed that minor differences in tonality could make a huge impact and that different colors could evoke different responses.

Setup for final line of essay.

In high school I moved on to more advanced projects, teaching myself how to take apart, repair, and customize cell phones. Whether I was adjusting the flex cords that connect the IPS LCD to the iPhone motherboard, or replacing the vibrator motor, I loved discovering the many engineering feats Apple overcame in its efforts to combine form with function.

And once I obtained my driver's license, I began working on cars. Many nights you'll find me in the garage replacing standard chrome trim with an elegant piano black finish or changing the threads on the stitching of the seats to add a personal touch, as I believe a few small changes can transform a generic product into a personalized work of art.

Note this paragraph ends with a nice "so what" insight.

Again, core values—good with hands, attention to aesthetics— followed by a "so what" insight.

My love of details applies to my schoolwork too.

I'm the math geek who marvels at the fundamental theorems of Calculus, or who sees beauty in A = (s(s − a)(s − b)(s − c))^(1 / 2). Again, it's in the details: one bracket off or one digit missing and the whole equation collapses. And details are more than details, they can mean the difference between negative and positive infinity, an impossible range of solutions.

I also love sharing this appreciation with others and have taken it upon myself to personally eradicate mathonumophobiconfundosis, my Calculus teacher's term for "extreme fear of Math." A small group of other students and I have devoted our after-school time to tutoring our peers in everything from Pre-Algebra to AP Calculus B/C and I believe my fluency in Hebrew and Farsi has helped me connect with some of my school's Israeli and Iranian students. There's nothing better than seeing a student solve a difficult problem without me saying anything.

Core value: helping others. And another subtle brag (see page 119).

You probably think I want to be a designer. Or perhaps an engineer?

Wrong. Well, kind of.

Actually, I want to study Endodontics, which is (I'll save you the Wikipedia look-up) a branch of dentistry that deals with the tooth pulp and the tissues surrounding the root of a tooth. As an Endodontist, I'll be working to repair damaged teeth by performing precision root canals and implementing dental crowns. Sound exciting? It is to me.

The fact is, it's not unlike the work I've been doing repairing cellphone circuits and modifying cars, though there is one small difference. In the future I'll still be working to repair machines, but this machine is one of the most sophisticated machines ever created: the human body. Here, my obsession with details will be as crucial as ever. A one millimeter difference can mean the difference between a successful root canal and a lawsuit.

The question is: Will the toothbrushes I hand out be mineral white or diamond white?

The ending is surprising, but inevitable. See page 150 for more.

This call-back to earlier in the essay helps us feel like we've come full circle.

TYPE C: "RAISING ANTHONY"

Written by a student who did **face significant challenges, and** did not know **what she wanted to study**

Again, narrative structure works well when relating challenges.

At age three, I was separated from my mother. The court gave full custody of both my baby brother and me to my father. Of course, at my young age, I had no clue what was going on. However, it did not take me long to realize that life with my father would not be without its difficulties.

My brother, Anthony, was eleven months old when my father placed us in the hands of our first babysitter. I remember being confused at first, wondering where my father had gone and when he would be back, but after a while, I became accustomed to this routine of absence and the never ending babysitters that

Inciting incident: we get why this might be the worst thing that could happen, so no need for status quo.

filled in for him. These strangers consisted of college students, chain-smokers, senile women, and foreigners—all were technically adults, but not one was a suitable substitute for a parent.

Raise the stakes: not just bad babysitters, but absent father, too.
When my father was home, he still seemed absent; he was distant both physically and emotionally. He was busy bouncing from one girlfriend to the next, sleeping in until 1:30 in the afternoon, and sitting on the couch watching television. He took us out to restaurants every night and wasted the money he earned on expensive dinners, his current girlfriend, and liquor. This continued for ten years.

Raise the stakes even more: ten years is a long time.
Legally, we had all the necessities to survive, but in truth our home was devoid of structure. Schoolwork went unchecked. Bedtimes were unregulated. Dust accumulated in thick layers on the paperwork that overflowed on the dining table. Often times, Anthony and I would spend hours waiting at school for someone to pick us up, and most of our dinners were served well past eleven at night.
Raise the stakes yet again: even more challenges.

What she did about it: Part 1.
Consequentially, and quite unwittingly, I shed my childhood and assumed the role of "parent" for Anthony before my seventh birthday. I memorized the routes we took to school and led Anthony home myself. I watched professional chefs on PBS and learned how to cook basic meals for two. Unfortunately, as I progressively developed into the parent, Anthony took advantage of our lack of true authority and grew into the epitome of a problem child. He became unruly, and his behavior soon bled into his school life. His grades suffered and he seemed to act

This is the lowest point of the story, or what the late screenwriting guru Blake Snyder used to call "Dark Night of the Soul."
out more often. His rash temper continued to grow until one day the school called our home because he had tried to throw a chair at his teacher.
Anthony was the only kindergartner in our school's history to be suspended. The school counselor recommended that when my father was in town we attend therapy as a family. But that accomplished nothing—my father's initial attempts to

implement authority devolved quickly into apathy, and then he was traveling again. I, on the other hand, would not give up so easily. I became the watchful eye and mentor that Anthony and I both needed. I soaked in the parenting videos that our family counselor had given my dad. I explained to Anthony why a structured lifestyle is important and why retribution is needed for one's misdeeds. To further instill self-discipline in him, I would have him formulate his own penalties. I also began to follow up on his schoolwork by contacting his teachers.

What she did about it: Part 2.

On one particularly hopeful afternoon I even tried to introduce him to books that I had read—but I learned I can't win every battle. I wasn't satisfied with just giving a fish to my little brother; I wanted to teach him how to cast lines himself and learn the tools of self-reliance. Looking back at my hectic childhood, I am grateful for the insight it afforded me, and I am grateful for the effect my little brother had on me.

Great verisimilitude: a detail that makes this feel like real life (see page 147 for more).

Inadvertently, by raising Anthony I ended up raising myself. Living with my unreliable father and reliant younger brother gave me the need and incentive to find myself and to mature quickly. At a very early age I became resourceful, independent, and responsible. It makes me proud to know that I single-handedly raised Anthony and myself. I now know that I can face any challenge with confidence. Even if I don't succeed, I know I will be stronger just for trying.

She clarifies her core values here, which she'll carry with her to college and beyond.

Remember that montage structure works well for this type of essay.

TYPE D: "SCRAPBOOK"

Written by a student who** did not **face significant challenges and** did not know **what she wanted to study

I look at the ticking, white clock: it's eleven at night, my prime-time. I clear the carpet of the Sony camera charger, the faded Levi's, and last week's Statistics homework. Having prepared my workspace, I pull out two 12 by 12 crème sheets and reproduce sketches of the layouts already imprinted in my head. Now I can really begin.

I leave a quarter inch border as I cut the first photograph, which I then adhere to a polka-dotted paper. For a sophisticated touch, I use needle and thread to sew the papers together. Loads of snipping and pasting later, the clock reads three in the morning. I glance down at the final product and feel an overwhelming sense of pride as I brush my fingers over the many layers and pages. For me, the act of taking pieces of my life and putting them together on a page is my way of organizing remnants of my past to make something whole and complete. This particular project is the most valuable one to date: the scrapbook of my life.

Focusing lens is made clear here, giving us context for the upcoming montage. It's also her thesis.

In the center of the first page are the words MY WORLD in periwinkle letters. All four of my Korean grandparents sit in the top corner, looking over my first birthday—my ddol. Underneath them are my cousins trying not to let go of their overwhelming laughter while playing "red light, green light" at O'Melveney Park. Meanwhile, my Texas relatives watch Daniel, the youngest, throw autumn leaves into the air that someone had spent hours raking up. To the right, my friends miserably pose for our history teacher who documents our droopy faces the morning of our first AP exam. The largest photograph is that of my family huddled in front of the fireplace, drinking my brother's hot cocoa and listening to the pitter-patter of sporadic Los Angles rain.

Core value: family.

Again, note how each object (or detail) reveals important values: diversity, culture, adventure, openness.

I move over to the right side of the page. At the top, I have delicately sewn on three items. The first is a page of a Bible that was given to the soldiers at a Cambodian base where I taught English. Beneath is the picture of my group of Guatemalan girls devouring *arroz con pollo*, red sauce slobbered all over our lips. I reread the third item, a short note that a student of mine from a rural Korean school had struggled to write in her broken

Note how these essence objects— fireplace, brother's hot cocoa, sound of rain—reveal her family values: warmth, connection, intimacy.

English. Moving down the page, I see the shelf display of my vibrantly glazed ceramic projects. I have included a clipping of my page from the school newspaper, next to ticket stubs for Wicked from my date with Dad. I made sure to incorporate a snapshot of my first scrapbook page featuring a visit to Hearst Castle on my tenth birthday.

After proudly looking over each detail, I turn to the next page, which I've labeled: AND BEYOND. This page is not cluttered or crowded. There is my college diploma with International Relations listed and the school's name left blank. A map covers nearly half the paper with stickers pinpointing locations all over the world, but I cannot recognize the countries' names. The remainder of the page is a series of frames with captions underneath. Without the photographs, the descriptions are cryptic.

For now, that second page remains incomplete because I have no precise itinerary for my future. The red flags on the map represent the places I will travel to, possibly to teach English or to partner with a charity again. As for the empty frames, they will be filled with the people I will meet: a family of my own and the families I desire to help, through a career I have yet to adopt. Until these things unfold, all I can do is prepare. I'll continue to finalize the layout and gather materials so that I can start piecing together the next part, the next page of my life's scrapbook.

She's setting up her conclusion, which answers "so what?"

Note the metaphors. She'll explain these in a second, but first she shows them.

Values that will be important to her no matter what career she chooses: travel, teaching, family, helping others.

She returns to the opening image, which, as in the "Endodontics" essay, lends a feeling of closure.

CHAPTER FOUR

A Step-by-Step Guide to Writing Each of the Four College Essay Types

OKAY, HERE'S THE PART WHERE you get to choose your own adventure.

Take a look at the diagram below and pick the path that sounds the most interesting and applicable. Keep in mind that these are not types of students, since you could use any of these paths. These are simply four different ways to tell your story.

A	B
Student **has** faced significant challenges and **does know** what he or she wants to study.	Student **has not** faced significant challenges and **does know** what he or she wants to study.
C	D
Student **has** faced significant challenges and **does not know** what he or she wants to study.	Student **has not** faced significant challenges and **does not know** what he or she wants to study.

For type A, turn to page 40.
For type B, turn to page 59.
For type C, turn to page 71.
For type D, turn to page 89.

If you're not sure yet, or want to see what each method has to offer, read through them all. One benefit of understanding all four methods is that you'll be able to combine elements of them to create your own.

All right, heeeeeeere we go.

HOW TO WRITE ESSAY TYPE A

For Students Who *Have* Faced Significant Challenges and *Do Know* What They Want to Study

You may be wondering: What counts as a "significant" challenge? Who decides? The answer is simple:

You decide what counts as a significant challenge.

But maybe you'd like some ideas. No problem.

A List of Challenges You Might Discuss in Your Essay

- single-parent household
- significant work hours while in high school, particularly if you contributed to the family income to help pay bills
- low-income family or large family with many dependents
- you're the first person in your family to attend college
- parents' disability or unemployment (specify what and how long)
- any physical or learning disabilities (diagnosed by a health professional; specify what and how long)
- language spoken at home other than English or any portion of your high school career that was taken outside of the United States

IMPORTANT NOTE: You don't *have* to write about these things in your main essay.

If you have faced significant challenges, this information could also be included in the additional information section or elsewhere in your application—and your challenge certainly doesn't have to dominate your essay. For example, if there are any potential red flags on your application (low grades, classes or activities dropped, important school changes), explanations for them can be mentioned in your additional information section or *very* briefly in your main essay, but your whole essay should not be solely about your grades or school change—you'll want to discuss those challenges in the context of a broader, more meaningful story.

ANOTHER IMPORTANT NOTE: If you don't believe you've experienced significant challenges, or if you believe you've been through "some stuff" but you're not sure that "stuff" would qualify as a "significant challenge," you can still use this type A step-by-step approach to write your essay—simply replace the word "challenge" or "challenges" in the following paragraphs with the word "experience" or "experiences."

Let's get to it.

THE SECRET TO WRITING ESSAY TYPE A

If you **have faced** significant challenges in your life and you **do know** what you want to study, the key question for your essay is this:

How do the challenges from my past connect to my future career?

And the secret is...

Through your values.

What do I mean? This:

1. You experienced **challenges**.
2. Those challenges had particular **effects** or repercussions, impacting you in a variety of ways.
3. To get through those challenges, **you took action**.
4. As a result, you developed certain resources, skills, or **values**.
5. And the resources, skills, and values you developed as a result of your challenges will serve you in [insert chosen **career** here].

Visually speaking, that looks something like this:

Challenges   Effects   What You Did   Values   Career

HOW TO CONNECT YOUR CHALLENGES TO YOUR INTENDED CAREER

Get out a blank sheet of paper, turn it sideways (horizontally), and write these words along the top:

1. Challenges	2. Effects	3. What I Did	4. Values	5. Amazing [insert chosen career here] (Doctor, Artist, and so on)

HERE'S WHAT TO WRITE IN EACH COLUMN:

Column 1: Challenges

What difficulties did you face or are you currently facing?

Feel free to list several. Perhaps not all of these challenges will end up in the essay, but we're just brainstorming right now, so at this point, list all that come to mind. Even write the one that feels edgy to talk about, that you think, "Nah, that's too personal." Write that one down, too, just for the sake of the exercise.

If you're wondering if any topics are off-limits or how much sharing is too much, see pages 75 and 76.

Examples of Challenges

❏ adapting to a new culture in a new country
❏ moving a lot and having no real place to call home

❏ divorce

❏ being afraid to come out as lesbian, gay, bisexual, transgender, queer

❏ having an extremely shy personality

❏ having to work to pay for groceries

❏ dealing with the death of a family member

❏ adjusting to a new school

❏ parents or siblings fighting a lot

❏ parents not being home a lot

❏ racism

❏ crime

❏ school or neighborhood violence

❏ failing to meet someone's expectations

❏ alcohol or drug abuse

❏ joblessness or unemployment

❏ illness (you or someone close to you)

❏ failure

❏ natural disaster (hurricane, earthquake)

❏ car crash

❏ war

❏ riots

❏ home invasion or break-in

❏ fire

❏ ignorance

❏ physical injury

❏ physical disability

❏ mental illness

❏ suicide

❏ sibling rivalry

❏ getting rejected

❏ a learning difference or disability

❏ sexism

❏ abuse

❐ controlling behavior from family or friends
❐ dealing with an excessively critical person
❐ aggression
❐ cruelty
❐ destructive behavior/bullying/cyberbullying
❐ peer pressure
❐ discrimination based on being a minority (race, sexual orientation, nationality, and so on)
❐ lack of access to educational resources
❐ parents not supportive of your dreams

Column 2: Effects

What negative effects did you experience as a result of your challenges? (Note that you probably experienced some positive effects, too, but save those for the fourth column.)

The purpose of this section is to differentiate *your* experiences from those of everyone else who went through (and is writing his or her college essay about) the challenges you faced.

For example, Student A and Student B might both write "my dad lost his job" as a challenge. However, for Student A, the effects might have been "domestic violence," "poverty," and "mom left us," whereas for Student B, the effects might have been "sleepless nights" and "we had to sell one of our cars."

Two important things to remember as you're brainstorming this section:

1. You don't need to match just one effect per challenge—one challenge can have several repercussions.
2. This part of the process can take some time, so be patient.

Column 3: What I Did

What actions did you take to change or improve your situation?

Examples: I started helping out more around the house; I got a part-time job; I quit Key Club, SADD, and French Club; or I secretly went into my brother's room and folded his unkempt pajamas.

In the third column, list all the positive actions you took.

Column 4: Values

What qualities/skills/values/resources did you develop during this time?

For ideas and examples, go back to the Core Values Exercise on page 8, but this time—rather than thinking of your core values—consider which values you developed as a result of the experiences you listed in the third column.

Make that list now.

Here's an example of how your brainstorm page may be shaping up. (Note that I list only one challenge, while you might list several.)

1. Challenges	2. Effects	3. What I Did	4. Values	5. Amazing [Doctor]
mom lost her job	no money	got a job	accountability	
			confidence	
			beauty	
	dad worked more	taught myself to cook	health	
			art	
	had to quit soccer	play w/ brothers	gratitude	
			listening	

IMPORTANT NOTE: See if you can include several *unexpected* connections or values. In the example, many of the connections between the "what I did" and the "values" are pretty obvious. But a few are not so obvious, such as the connections between how "[getting] a job" led to the value of "beauty" or how "[teaching] myself to cook" might lead to "art." It's these unusual values—or usual values developed in unusual ways—that can lead to unique insights and make your essay stand out.

And the point I just made is so important that I feel I must underscore it:

If you use only predictable values at the end of your essay and explain your values in usual ways, there is a good chance your essay will be boring.

- Examples of predictable values gained from working a job: discipline, commitment, hard work
- Examples of less predictable values gained from working a job: risk, social change, healthy boundaries

Which group of values makes for a more interesting essay? That's a rhetorical question, but just in case: the second group. Just to get your brain turning, here are a couple more examples:

- Predictable values gained from teaching yourself to cook: responsibility, health, helping others
- Less predictable values gained from teaching yourself to cook: art, privacy, practicality

IMPORTANT NOTE: Just because the values are predictable doesn't mean that they are wrong or boring or that you are wrong or boring. I've read great essays that have used predictable values, but here's the key: the more usual the values are, the more well-crafted (or unusual) the "so what" moments need to be. Look at the "With Debate" (page 22) or "Stomach Whisperer" (page 69) essays—in both of these, the authors developed confidence (which could be called a "predictable" value), but how the confidence was developed was told in an interesting and somewhat unusual way.

Also, just because you choose to write about unusual values doesn't mean you should necessarily use such words in a straightforward and direct way. In other words, I wouldn't recommend saying, "Teaching myself to cook taught me the values of art, privacy, and practicality." That can be really boring, too. Instead, show first how you developed the value, and then tell us anything else we might need to know or give us insight into why it was meaningful.

HOW CAN YOU BRAINSTORM LESS PREDICTABLE VALUES?

Try this: look at the Core Values Exercise on page 8 and see if you can choose a value you think will surprise me. (Yes, me, Ethan.) Imagine we're actually sitting across from each other and you've just told me about your challenge and what you did about it. Then pick a value on that list and imagine telling me what you gained from it. If you think I'll be able to guess the connection, chances are it'll be predictable for the reader. So pick something else. Keep going until you find something that you don't think I'd be able to guess right away.

Column 5: Amazing [Insert Chosen Career Here]

Ask yourself: What are the essential qualities of an amazing [whatever you want to be/study]? Don't worry about connecting these qualities to your values yet—we'll get there. Right now just list three to five essential qualities of someone who would be excellent in your potential future profession.

And, just as I've suggested earlier, make sure to not only include expected values, but also unusual values—values you wouldn't normally associate with that career. Consider that most essays on becoming a doctor, for example, will emphasize the value of "helping others." But what unusual values would you bring to the profession?

- Examples of predictable values in a doctor essay: responsibility, helping others, collaboration
- Examples of less predictable values in a doctor essay: laughter, restraint, balance

Will the reader be able to guess how those last values apply to being a doctor? Maybe, but at least you'd be making him or her do a little work. Think of the difference between a bad joke and a good one. If the punch line is predictable, the joke isn't funny. But if your brain has to do a little work, it's funnier. Usually.

Remember: The values *on their own* don't have to be strange or unusual; it can be the connection you make to the career that's unusual, as in the doctor examples. By this, I mean that "laughter" isn't on its own a weird value—it's just not likely to be the first value that comes to mind when you think of "doctor" and may be interesting to include in an essay that otherwise focuses solely on helping others.

If this is still unclear, the following essay is a quick example of a student who developed five values from playing a musical instrument. But, before you read it, try imagining what values most musical instrument essays focus on. In my experience, most of those essays focus on hard work, perseverance, excellence, and so on. But notice how this student doesn't focus on any of those.

"SANTUR"
150-word extracurricular statement

I've devoted thousands of hours to playing the santur, a classical Persian instrument that originated in the Middle East. Some think I'm strange: a Persian redheaded Jewish teenager obsessed with an ancient musical instrument. But many don't see what I see. My santur is King David's lyre: it can soothe, enrapture, mesmerize. It's also a tool for social change: many view Iran as a land of terrorists, but when I play, if just for a moment, the barrier is broken and the innocent of Iran, the educated, the artists, the innovators, come to life. The santur is also my way of connecting to my Persian grandfather, who was afflicted with Alzheimer's. In December I'll be releasing my first album and donating the proceeds to Alzheimer's research, doing my part to help eradicate the disease and preserve the voice of the santur so that it shall never be forgotten.

I count at least five values in 148 words. Pretty good.

So first ask yourself: What are the essential qualities of an amazing [insert chosen career here]? Write them down. Then ask: What will my secret sauce be? What, in other words, will make you (and your essay) different from all the other future doctors (and future doctor application essays)?

At this point, your brainstorm page might look something like this:

1. Challenges	2. Effects	3. What I Did	4. Values	5. Amazing [Doctor]
mom lost her job	no money	got a job	accountability	listening
			confidence	restraint
			beauty	improvisation
	dad worked more	taught myself to cook	health	efficiency
			art	accountability
	had to quit soccer	play w/ brothers	gratitude	fun
			listening	

Note that some of your values in the fourth column (Values) may overlap with the values in your fifth column (Amazing [Career]), and some may not. That's okay. You don't have to connect all the values right now, and you certainly don't have to use everything you've written down. At this point, we're still brainstorming.

What to do next:

START MAKING SOME CONNECTIONS

Here's the fun part. See if you notice any threads of connection between the challenges, effects, what you did, values you developed, and the qualities necessary to be a great [whatever you want to be].

You can even draw some arrows to help you see the connections. Note that if you spot a continuous thread of connection from the first column to the fifth column, that's great, as this could provide the connective thread for your entire story.

Example 1:
(Challenges, Effects, What I Did, Values, and Career are marked in bold.)

> I noticed that after **my father lost his job** that's when he started **drinking** and becoming **verbally abusive** and my **grades went down** and I started to become **angry**. Deep down all I really wanted was a mentor and someone I could talk to. It wasn't until 9th grade when I joined **wrestling** that I found a way to channel my frustrations and anger. That's when things shifted for me, **my grades went up**, and, though we were never able to fully connect, my **father quit drinking**. Wrestling really turned things around for me: it taught me to **channel my emotions** in more productive ways, **manage my time**, and even **inspired me** to work with other young men to help them learn the value of **healthy competition**, potentially as a **coach**. I hope to one day be there for other young men to listen to them and provide the positive role model I never had.

IMPORTANT NOTE: You don't have to connect ALL your challenges to the qualities of a great [whatever you want to be]. Try to find just two or three connective threads. Why? Because not all your great qualities were born from struggle—some were born out of curiosity or your innate awesomeness. So just try to make a few connections now. It's almost time to start writing.

WHAT NOW?

Here are a few options:

Option 1: Just write a draft.

That's right. You've got the content and you've identified a couple connective threads: jump in and start writing while you're inspired. (Tip: If you wait twenty-four hours, chances are you'll have forgotten some of the connections your brain just made—it starts to fade fast, like a dream—so capture the ideas now in a rough draft.)

Option 2: Read "How to Write Essay Type C" in this chapter for more tips on writing about challenges.

This section, which begins on page 71, is especially useful if you're interested in writing about challenges, but you're uncertain about your career path. It also answers "Are any topics off-limits?" and "How much sharing is too much?"

Option 3 (my favorite): Add emotional depth and layers by completing the Feelings and Needs Exercise.

For this, turn to the "How Do I Make My Essay, Like, Deep?" section on page 121.

Option 4: Create a simple three-part challenges essay outline using these elements:

1. Challenges and effects ($\approx$ 1/3 of essay)
2. What I did ($\approx$ 1/3 of essay)

3. What I learned that led me to discover my calling ($\approx$ 1/3 of essay)

Note that sometimes it's difficult to get all the challenges into the first third. If so, make sure you at least get the challenges into the first half of your essay. But I'd recommend including a turning point (a.k.a. what you did about it) before the middle of the essay.

If it helps, give yourself a word budget. Say, for example, you're writing a 650-word essay. If so, that's:

1. Challenges and effects: 216.66 words
2. What I did: 216.66 words
3. What I learned that led me to discover my calling: 216.66 words

Must your essay follow this budget precisely? Of course not. That ".66 words" thing is a joke: How could you possibly write just part of a word? This is simply a rough guide for how much space you should spend on each part. But with this simple three-part structure, you should be able to start your essay.

Want a more in-depth outline?

Option 5: Use narrative structure to create your outline.
Note that this will work best after completing the Feelings and Needs Exercise mentioned in Option 3.

As a reminder, here are the six elements of narrative structure:

1. **Inciting Incident**: What moment or event launched your story? Often it's the worst thing that could have happened.
2. **Status Quo**: What do we need to know in order to understand why the inciting incident was the worst thing that could have happened to you? (Note that in the discussion of narrative structure on page 14, status quo is listed before inciting incident, but often it can be more exciting to switch the order. Remember: It's art, not science. If your inciting incident comes

first, your status quo provides the context for the opening image or moment.)

3. **Raise the Stakes**: What happened to make things worse, more important, serious, or dangerous? What else happened?
4. **Turning Point**: When did things shift? Often this involves a choice that you made, perhaps a decision to take action.
5. **Denouement**: What did you do about it?
6. **New Status Quo**: How are things different now from the original status quo?

Think of each of these parts as a paragraph. Then write your essay draft.

Note: Once you've written a draft, turn to "How to Revise Your Essay in Five Steps" on page 102.

Want another example of narrative structure used to write essay type A?

Check out the "Porcelain God" essay that follows.

"PORCELAIN GOD"

Written by a student who did face significant challenges and did know what she wanted to study

Bowing down to the porcelain god, I emptied the contents of my stomach. Foaming at the mouth, I was ready to pass out. My body couldn't stop shaking as I gasped for air, and the room started spinning.

Ten minutes prior, I had been eating dinner with my family at a Chinese restaurant, drinking chicken-feet soup. My mom had specifically asked the waitress if there were peanuts in it, because when I was two we found out that I am deathly allergic to them. When the waitress replied no, I went for it. Suddenly I started scratching my neck, feeling the hives that had started to form. I rushed to the restroom to throw up because my throat was itchy and I felt a weight on my chest. I was experiencing anaphylactic shock, which prevented me from taking anything but shallow breaths. I was fighting the one thing that is meant to protect me and keep me alive—my own body.

At five years old, I couldn't comprehend what had happened. All I knew was that I felt sick, and I was waiting for my mom to give me something to make it better. I thought my parents were superheroes; surely they would be able to make me well again. But I became scared when I heard the fear in their voices as they rushed me to the ER.

After that incident, I began to fear. I became scared of death, eating, and even my own body. As I grew older, I became paranoid about checking food labels and I avoided eating if I didn't know what was in the food. I knew what could happen if I ate one wrong thing, and I wasn't willing to risk it for a snack. Ultimately, that fear turned into resentment; I resented my body for making me an outsider.

In the years that followed, this experience and my regular visits to my allergy specialist inspired me to become an allergy specialist. Even though I was probably only ten at the time, I wanted to find a way to help kids like me. I wanted to find a solution so that nobody would have to feel the way I did; nobody deserved to feel that pain, fear, and resentment. As I learned more about the medical world, I became more fascinated with the body's immune responses, specifically, how a body reacts to allergens. This past summer, I took a month-long course on human immunology at Stanford University. I learned about the different mechanisms and cells that our bodies use in order to fight off pathogens. My desire to major in biology in college has been stimulated by my fascination with the human body, its processes, and the desire to find a way to help people with allergies. I hope that one day I can find a way to stop allergic reactions or at least lessen the symptoms, so that children and adults don't have to feel the same fear and bitterness that I felt.

Note how the author's allergic reaction, brought on by anaphylactic shock (**Challenge**), led her to fear death, eating, and even her own body (**Effects**). This led her to a desire for knowledge about the body's immune responses and its reaction to allergens, which led her to take the course at Stanford (**What She Did**), and ultimately inspired her to become an allergy specialist (**Career**) so that children and adults don't have to feel the same fear and bitterness that she felt (**Values**). Note, too, that in her essay, she mentions her career before she mentions her values, which of course is fine. The brainstorming columns provided earlier aren't a mandate on how you must order everything in your essay. That goes for everything in this book, by the way: take these tools and make your essay your own.

> Fun fact: The admissions officers at Davidson College liked this essay so much that they asked the author if they could use it as a sample for how to write a great essay.

Here's one more type A essay example that illustrates narrative structure in a clear way:

"EASTER"
Written by a student who did *face significant challenges* and did know *what she wanted to study*

It was Easter and we should've been celebrating with our family, but my father had locked us in the house. If he wasn't going out, neither were my mother and I.

My mother came to the U.S. from Mexico to study English. She'd been an exceptional student and had a bright future ahead of her. But she fell in love and eloped with the man that eventually became my father. He loved her in an unhealthy way, and was both physically and verbally abusive. My mother lacked the courage to start over so she stayed with him and slowly let go of her dreams and aspirations. But she wouldn't allow for the same to happen to me.

In the summer before my junior year I was offered a scholarship to study abroad in Egypt. Not to my surprise, my father refused to let me go. But my mother wouldn't let him crush my dreams as well. I'd do this for myself and for my mother's unfulfilled aspirations. I accepted the scholarship.

I thought I'd finally have all the freedom I longed for in Egypt, but initially I didn't. On a weekly basis I heard insults and encountered harassment in the streets, yet I didn't yield to the societal expectations for women by staying indoors. I continued to roam throughout Egypt, exploring the Great Pyramids of Giza, cruising on the Nile, and traveling to Luxor and Aswan. And before I returned to the U.S. I received the unexpected opportunity to travel to London and Paris. It was surreal: a girl from the ghetto traveling alone around the world with a map in her hands and no man or cultural standards could dictate what I was to do. I rode the subway from Cambridge University to the British Museum. I took a train from London to Paris and in two days I visited the Eiffel Tower, the Louvre, Notre Dame Cathedral, and took a cruise on the Seine. Despite the language barrier I found I had the self-confidence to approach anyone for directions.

While I was in Europe enjoying my freedom, my mother moved out and rented her own place. It was as if we'd simultaneously gained our independence. We were proud of each other. And she vicariously lived through my experiences as I sent her pictures and told her about my adventures.

Finally, we were free.

I currently live in the U.S with my mother. My father has

gradually transformed from a frigid man to the loving father I had yearned for. Life isn't perfect, but for the moment I'm enjoying tranquility and stability with my family and are communicating much better than before.

I'm involved in my school's Leadership Council as leader of our events committee. We plan and execute school dances and create effective donation letters. I see this as a stepping-stone for my future, as I plan to double major in Women's Studies and International Relations with a focus on Middle Eastern studies. After the political turmoil of the Arab Spring many Middle Eastern countries refuse to grant women equal positions in society because that would contradict Islamic texts. By oppressing women they are silencing half of their population. I believe these Islamic texts have been misinterpreted throughout time, and my journey towards my own independence has inspired me to help other women find liberation as well.

My Easter will drastically differ from past years. Rather than being locked at home, my mother and I will celebrate outdoors our rebirth and renewal.

Note the narrative structure elements in this essay:

- **Inciting Incident**: Author and her mother are locked in the house by the author's father.
- **Status Quo** (which provides context): Father has been physically and verbally abusive for years, mother and daughter are trapped not only physically but psychologically. (Like the "Porcelain God" essay, the inciting incident comes first—that's the hook—then we get some background details.)
- **Raise the Stakes**: Author is offered a scholarship to study in Egypt and father initially won't let her go. We wonder: What will happen?

- **Turning Point 1**: Her mother gives her permission, and author accepts the scholarship.
- **Raise the Stakes Even More**: Rather than experiencing freedom in Egypt, author experiences sexism.
- **Turning Point 2**: Author describes the surreal experience of exploring Europe: "a girl from the ghetto traveling alone around the world with a map in her hands and no man or cultural standards could dictate what [she] was to do" (this line always makes me cry). She gains confidence and independence and learns that mom has moved out, in effect gaining her own independence.
- **New Status Quo**: "Finally, we were free." After being oppressed by men for years, the author decides to major in women's studies. The final sentence returns to the opening, but rather than being locked inside her house, in the future the author and her mother "will celebrate outdoors [their] rebirth and renewal." Boom.

HOW TO WRITE ESSAY TYPE B

For students who *have not* faced significant challenges and *do know* what they want to study

THE SECRET TO WRITING THIS TYPE OF ESSAY

Write your essay backward.

One of my favorite ways to outline a type B essay is to "write it backward," which essentially involves reverse engineering the essay using montage structure. Here's how it works:

Turn a piece of paper sideways (horizontally) and write these headings along the top:

How I've Developed These Values	Essential Values of a Great [insert chosen career here]	Insights

HERE'S WHAT TO WRITE IN EACH COLUMN:

Center Column: Essential Values of a Great [Insert Chosen Career Here]

1. Make a list of the qualities necessary to excel in whichever field you've chosen. If, for example, you want to study business, you might write "resourcefulness" or "autonomy" on your list.

Tip: Brainstorm several unusual values. "Helping others" may be a common value for a doctor, for example, whereas "creativity" or "restraint" may be less common. Or "efficiency" might be common in an engineering essay, whereas "fun" or "beauty" may be less common.

If you're having trouble coming up with a list, refer to the Core Values Exercise on page 8.

Another tip: You may want to do some research by asking a few people in your chosen field, "What's amazing about your job?" or "Why do you do what you do?" Note that phrasing your questions in this way might be more effective at eliciting values than asking a question like, "What are the necessary skills required of your career?" Why? You're not looking for what is most logical (head), but for purpose and meaning (heart). In other words: not *what*, but *why*. So phrase your question in a way that invites deeper reflection. Other possibilities are, "What would I find surprising about your work?" or "Why are you great at what you do?"

List at least five qualities in the center column. Challenge yourself to identify at least two unusual ones.

Left Column: How I've Developed These Values

1. For each quality in your center column, write a specific moment or example from your life that SHOWS that you've developed this quality. (For example, if you wrote "ability to work well with others" in your center column, write a specific instance that shows you work well with others—like the time you worked with a large group to organize the Dance Marathon at your school. Or if you wrote "good listener" in the center column, you might describe how, while volunteering at the hospital, you found that the patients often felt comfortable sharing their life stories with you.)
2. Keep going until the left column is filled with examples that demonstrate the qualities you've listed in the center column.

Here's an example of what your brainstorm might look like so far, based on the "Endodontics" essay on page 24:

How I've Developed These Values	Essential Values of a Great Endodontist	Insights
After-school math tutoring	Desire to help others	
Designing my own shoes	Detail-focused	
Taking apart machines	Interested in how human body works	
Always asked questions as a kid	Curiosity	

After you've finished the steps above, you'll have your basic outline. But there's one more part left to brainstorm, and it's key to making your essay stand out.

Right Column: Insights

An insight is something you know or see that another person may not. Why are moments of insight important in your essay? Because, if you describe the examples you've brainstormed in a simple and straightforward way, your essay might still sound a little flat or boring. You need insights, or what I call "so what" moments. So...

For each of your examples, write down a particular lesson or skill you learned that is beyond what the average person knows. How do you do this? Think about your example and simply ask yourself, "So what?" Then ask yourself, "So what?" again. Keep going to see where it leads.

Here are some examples from the "Endodontics" essay (and I've highlighted the insight/"so what" moments in bold):

> In high school I moved on to more advanced projects, teaching myself how to take apart, repair, and customize cell phones. Whether I was adjusting the flex cords that connect the IPS LCD

to the iPhone motherboard, or replacing the vibrator motor, **I loved discovering the many engineering feats Apple overcame in its efforts to combine form with function.**

And once I obtained my driver's license, I began working on cars. Many nights you'll find me in the garage replacing standard chrome trim with an elegant piano black finish or changing the threads on the stitching of the seats to add a personal touch, **as I believe a few small changes can transform a generic product into a personalized work of art.**

My love of details applies to my schoolwork too.

I'm the math geek who marvels at the fundamental theorems of Calculus, or who sees beauty in $A = (s(s - a)(s - b)(s - c))^{\wedge}(1 / 2)$. Again, **it's in the details: one bracket off or one digit missing and the whole equation collapses. And details are more than details, they can mean the difference between negative and positive infinity, an impossible range of solutions.**

Notice how each of these "so what" moments tells us something the reader probably wouldn't have been able to come up with on his or her own. These moments illuminate the author's unique perspective. For more on this, see "Analogy of the Painter, the Art Critic, and the Curator" on page 117.

ONE FINAL IMPORTANT NOTE: Be patient with this "insight" part. It's the toughest part of the essay, and you may not discover your "so what" moments until later in the writing process. You can either start writing before you have all the insights figured out, hoping to discover them along the way, or figure out the insights before you start a draft—either can work.

When you're ready to start writing, here are a few tips.

TIPS FOR WRITING A TYPE B ESSAY

1. Before you begin, decide on an order for your examples. One way might be chronologically—in other words, the order in which you developed the values.

2. Think of the first two-thirds or three-fourths of the essay as the "show," full of images, essence objects, and details that illustrate your values—but don't make the values too obvious or you might make the ending obvious. For example, suppose your essay opens with "I've always wanted to be a doctor." If your first paragraph is about how your father is a doctor (value: family), your second paragraph is about how your favorite class is anatomy (value: knowledge), and your third paragraph is about volunteering at your local hospital (value: helping others), then the ending better be about how you want to be a chef or sports agent (which all those values will work for, by the way). If your ending is "I want to be a doctor," then we're in trouble. And by "in trouble," I just mean bored. (For tips on avoiding being predictable, check out Advanced Technique 4 on how to blow the reader's mind by using *The Sixth Sense* ending on page 150.)

3. At some point—perhaps two-thirds or three-fourths of the way through the essay—you'll probably want to mention your potential career.

4. Think of the last one-third or one-fourth of the essay as the "tell," in which you help the reader make connections between the values you've shown and what you'd like to study.

5. Remember that montage structure works well for a type B essay. For a very clear example, check out the "Endodontics" essay on page 24. For another, check out the "Behavioral Economics" essay that follows.

WHAT NOW?

1. Brainstorm the qualities or values that will make you amazing at your career.
2. Come up with an example demonstrating how you've developed each quality or value.
3. Brainstorm insights you've developed based on each of the values (see examples of this in the "Endodontics" essay).
4. Focus on one major example/value/insight per paragraph (of course there can be multiple examples, values, or insights if they are short, but it's easiest to focus on one per paragraph).
5. Near the end of the essay, reveal what you want to study and perhaps say why.
6. Once you've written a draft, turn to page 102 to learn how to revise your essay in five steps.

"BEHAVIORAL ECONOMICS"

Written by a student who did not face significant challenges and did know what he wanted to study

Fact: my grandfather got Jack Ruby off of his death sentence. He also got murderer Nathan Leopold paroled.

When I learned this as a sixth grader, I couldn't comprehend why my benevolent Grandpa Elmer would fight so hard for the lives of two killers. My grandma Midge explained to me that my grandpa "would rather let a guilty man go free than have an innocent man wrongfully imprisoned," and by preventing people from being executed, he adhered to this philosophy.

That was my first lesson in behavioral economics: trade-offs are necessary for a just society.

An experience with my Dad taught me my second lesson.

As a young man, my Dad had trouble finding an activity

he liked, until he picked up the bass guitar. From that point on, he immersed himself in music, eventually earned a jazz scholarship, secured a PhD, and became a sociology professor. And to this day, my Dad insists that the work ethic and focus he developed through music helped him find the career he loves.

But, I'm different. I love football.

Unfortunately, my Dad always considered football a waste of time and, after my parents' divorce, he threatened to make me quit. But through football I'd met some of my best friends, developed confidence, and grown closer with my younger brothers.

So, to prove to him that football wasn't a waste of time, I worked extra hard in the classroom, and in the weight room, almost as if my football career depended on it—which it did. Eventually, my efforts led to me winning an all-Greater Spokane League first team academic award for having the highest GPA of any senior on my team.

When I got home from the awards banquet, a realization hit me: my Dad's initial disapproval had fueled me to work as hard as I had. So, ironically, winning that football award was an indirect result of my Dad's first moment with his guitar.

This was my second lesson in behavioral economics: dramatic events often have distant, even subtle causes.

But it wasn't until I read *Freakonomics* that I began to actively examine the world through the lens of a behavioral economist.

While mentoring Keaziah, an at-risk fourth grader at an elementary school in a rough part of town, I subconsciously used a lesson I learned from *Freakonomics* to mentor him more effectively. Keaziah would not respond to the structured activities instituted by the mentorship program: he was reticent to paint birdhouses, for example, or play board games with the others. Instead of insisting that he partake in the usual methodical activities, however, I had a different idea. I began to take him to the basketball court, or to the computer lab, where a lack of structure enabled him to open up to me more naturally.

I realized that conventional wisdom was not always correct because, as *Freakonomics* taught me, irrationality is paradoxically one of the main constants to be expected in human behavior, rather than easily predictable rationality.

Behavioral economics has provided me with an avenue to explore some of life's most complex questions: How does one judge if a trade-off ultimately benefits society as a whole? And how does one balance autonomy with the desires of an important family member?

Although there are no concrete answers to these questions, finding my passion for the social sciences has not only led me to a potential career path, but also has brought me closer to my family. I now have a better understanding of who my Grandpa Elmer was, while my dad and I have found something in common: appreciation for the social sciences.

Although my Dad and I never had the clichéd father-son bonding moment while tossing the football in the backyard, our dinner-time discussions about current socioeconomics and extensive talks about the difference between neoclassical and behavioral economics have created even more quintessential moments between a Dad and son.

Note the simple framing device the author uses: three lessons from behavioral economics that relate to his own life. As he lays out each lesson, he reveals several core values, saving the insight/"so what" moment for the end of each section, which gives a "surprising but inevitable" quality, something I discuss more on page 150. The ending also doesn't tie things up neatly, but instead acknowledges that, while his relationship with his father is complex, it has evolved from the old status quo (Dad and I are different) to the new status quo

(Dad and I now have something in common), which is an example of using a narrative structure element in an essay that largely employs montage structure.

HOW TO COMBINE NARRATIVE AND MONTAGE STRUCTURES

It's perfectly possible to use elements of both the structures we've discussed, as you'll see in the "Stomach Whisperer" essay that follows. As you read it, try to identify elements from each type of structure. As a quick reminder, they are:

Narrative Structure (generally recommended for type A and C essays):
♦   Inciting incident/Status quo change
♦   Status quo
♦   Raise the stakes
♦   Turning point/Moment of truth
♦   Denouement/The final act
♦   Outcome/New status quo

Montage Structure (generally recommended for type B and D essays): finding a focusing lens that organizes the elements of your essay (and by "elements" I mean all the stuff you want to say about yourself) under a common theme.

What qualities or values will serve this student in her future career, and how did she develop them? (Hint: I spot at least six.)

"STOMACH WHISPERER"

Written by a student who did not *face significant challenges and* did know *what she wanted to study*

I could taste tangy cinnamon, a dash of extra vanilla, the raw flavor of molasses, all overlaid with the smooth creamy base of buttermilk batter. I'd just eaten my first bite of my grandmother's spice cake. That night, I lay with my ear against her stomach, listening to her digestion as she told me a bedtime story. Drowsily, I wondered if the echoing gurgle I'd just heard was caused by the molasses or by the cinnamon.

In the ensuing years, I never thought too much about the days when I was the Stomach Whisperer. Cooking everything I could get a recipe for, and navigating by trial and error where no recipes were found, I took advantage of my ability to pick out ingredients in what I ate. Gradually, that early curiosity regarding the destiny of what we eat soon evolved into an intense love of science.

In high school, I fed my interest in science. Classes like Biology weren't simply lectures designed to drill knowledge into my head; they were an experience. What I learned in science became intermingled with how I saw my environment; I could clearly picture my surroundings as the sum of billions of cells working together, or grasp how nitrogen fixation fit into the biogeochemical cycle.

But regardless of my new curiosity about science, I tended to second guess myself, especially during labs. A snarky voice inside me whispered that I couldn't find success in science if I had no self-confidence, or if I kept questioning whether or not I was doing a lab right. Tentative goals were forming in my mind, visions of a white coat with my name embossed on it, but I told myself that becoming a doctor was a ridiculous aspiration for a cook.

Abruptly, during junior year, my beliefs about my scientific capabilities underwent a metamorphosis. I was introduced to a new type of lab: specimen dissections. Lab handouts were scarce on instructions; once we delved into the anatomy of the stomach, they became little more than pictorial references. When asked to obtain a sample of stomach epithelium, I could make a lateral incision along the pylorus of the stomach or choose to slice open the fundus along the greater curvature. I was gleefully awed. Not only was I exploring the organ that I found most interesting, but I was actually doing a good job at it. No matter which way I chose to dissect, my eyes were opened to the fact that I had the capacity to be an independent thinker, someone who didn't necessarily need the instructions.

Armed with a newfound degree of self-assurance, I applied and was accepted to an internship at the Simi Dermatological Group. My assumption had been that when doctors see a patient, they deliberate briefly on treatment, and then prescribe whatever care is necessary. But interning showed me how very wrong I was. Patients came in daily with skin conditions that the doctors couldn't diagnose immediately. I saw that before they prescribed treatment, stellar doctors saw patients as a mixture of physical and mental parts, not just equations to plug various medicines into.

As a matter of fact, breaking a spice cake down to ingredients, I realized, isn't all that different from what a doctor does when diagnosing a patient. And in the future, I'll be combining cooking and science by becoming a gastroenterologist. With a wide array of gastric disorders to treat, from gastritis to polyps, I'll have to be self-assured, so my patients can get the best care possible. Still, each patient won't have a recipe that I can follow to cure them, so I'll draw on the thinking of the little girl in the kitchen, using what I know to make my own recipes. And simultaneously, I'll always be able to incorporate the mindset of the girl wondering whether cinnamon or molasses was the cause of that gastric condition.

In terms of montage structure, here are the qualities/values that will one day serve the author as a gastroenterologist, in the approximate order that they appear in the essay: **listening, curiosity, desire for knowledge, experience, lack of squeamishness** (I'm calling this a value since it's important for her career), **confidence, ability to improvise, willingness to take risks**.

In terms of narrative structure, the elements are: **status quo** (becoming a doctor was a ridiculous aspiration for a cook), **inciting incident** (during a dissection in class, she realized she didn't always need the instructions), **turning point** (she witnessed doctors solving problems without the instructions), **new status quo** (she realized that she could actually draw on her cooking background in the future as a gastroenterologist). Note that the author breaks the usual form by bringing up her main challenge later than usual—almost four paragraphs into the essay!—and then resolving it two paragraphs later. It works well, though, as it gives us a sense that her journey hasn't been without challenges. (Technically, this could also be considered a type A essay, but honestly, the exact type matters little—what's important is that the essay works.)

HOW TO WRITE ESSAY TYPE C

For students who *have* faced significant challenges and *do not know* what they want to study

Note: If you've already read "How to Write Essay Type A," you'll notice some of the following brainstorm instructions are similar, so feel free to skip those parts. But there are some differences in terms of how to structure and conclude your essay, so don't skip this section altogether, especially if you're contemplating *not* mentioning your potential future career at the end of your essay.

You may be wondering: What counts as a "significant" challenge? Who decides? The answer is simple:

You decide what counts as a significant challenge.

But maybe you'd like some ideas. No problem.

A List of Challenges You Might Discuss in Your Essay

- single-parent household
- significant work hours while in high school, particularly if you contributed to the family income to help pay bills
- low-income family or large family with many dependents
- you're the first person in your family to attend college
- parents' disability or unemployment (specify what and how long)
- any physical or learning disabilities (diagnosed by a health professional; specify what and how long)
- language spoken at home other than English, or any portion of your high school career that was taken outside of the United States

IMPORTANT NOTE: You don't *have* to write about these things in your main essay.

If you have faced significant challenges, this information could also be included in the additional information section or elsewhere in your application—and no single bullet point listed above has to dominate your essay. For example, if there are any potential red flags on your application (low grades, classes or activities dropped, important school changes), these can be mentioned in your additional information section or *very* briefly in your main essay, but your whole essay should not be solely about your grades or school change—you'll want to discuss those challenges in the context of a broader, more meaningful story.

ANOTHER IMPORTANT NOTE: If you don't believe you've experienced significant challenges, or if you believe you've been through some "stuff" but you're not sure that "stuff" would qualify as a "significant challenge," you can still use this type C step-by-step approach to write your essay—simply replace the word "challenge" or "challenges" in the following paragraphs with the word "experience" or "experiences."

THE SECRET TO WRITING ESSAY TYPE C

Be a victor, not a victim.

How?

a. Describe your challenges at the start of your essay, but don't dwell there.
b. Emphasize how you metabolized your challenges—in other words, what you did about them and what you learned.

The key to doing this well is to spend some serious time processing the "what I did" and "what I learned" and then to create for yourself a word budget that forces you to communicate your challenges in a succinct way. How do you do that? Read on.

HOW TO CONNECT YOUR CHALLENGES TO YOUR VALUES

STEP 1: BRAINSTORM THE CONTENT.

This, too, will be somewhat familiar if you've already read "How to Write Essay Type A." However, since you're not sure what you want to study, your essay won't make connections to your future career at the end of your essay. (Note: If you are sure, or have an idea about what you might like to study, read "How to Write Essay Type A" first, then this section.)

Here's a quick play-by-play:

1. You experienced **challenges**.
2. Those challenges had particular **effects** or repercussions, impacting you in a variety of ways.
3. To get through those challenges, you took **action**.
4. As a result, you developed certain resources, skills, or **values** that will be with you no matter what you study.

So the four questions for your essay are:

1. What **challenges** did you experience?
2. What **effects** did you face as a result of those challenges?
3. What did you **do** about it?
4. What **values** did you develop while working to overcome those challenges?

Challenges → Effects → What You Did → Values

To Organize Your Brainstorm, Do This:

Get out a blank sheet of paper, turn it sideways (horizontally), divide it into four columns, and label the columns like this:

1. Challenges	2. Effects	3. What I Did	4. Values

HERE'S WHAT TO WRITE IN EACH COLUMN:

Column 1: Challenges

What difficulties did you face or are you currently facing? Not sure what I mean by "challenges"? For examples, go to page 43.

Feel free to list several. Perhaps not all of these challenges will end up in the essay, but we're just brainstorming right now, so at this point, list all that come to mind. Even write the one that feels edgy to talk about, that you think, "Nah, that's too personal." Write that one down, too, just for the sake of the exercise.

FAQ

1. Are any topics off-limits?

Broadly speaking, very few topics are off-limits; it all depends on how the story is told. I've had students write about domestic violence, mental illness, and even self-harm in ways that have demonstrated vulnerability, core values, and insight.

The key question I always ask is this: Do you have enough distance and perspective on your challenge that you can articulate what you learned from the experience, or are you still so immersed in it that it's hard to speak about it with objectivity? *In other words, are you still in it, or have you come through it?*

If you've (honestly) come through it, then it could be worth writing about. But if you're still in it, or your essay deadline is looming, I recommend finding something else to write about. I say this because I've seen situations where students were trying to write on a tight deadline while dealing with a lot of feelings, and it just made them more stressed. But I've also seen situations where, even though a student was "in it" when they began their essay, the process of working on the essay—and in some cases, seeing a therapist—allowed the student to work through the experience and write about a sensitive challenge in a powerful way. However, this takes time.

REMEMBER: What is most interesting to a college is not your challenge, but how you metabolized your challenge—in other words, what you did about it and what you learned. If you have already metabolized/worked through your challenge, or you have time to, go for it. But if you don't, or you're afraid you might not, look for another topic.

Every situation is different, and if you're uncertain, please ask your counselor or a trusted mentor. Do make sure the person you're asking has had some experience advising students on topics for college admissions essays. And here's a tip: chances are, the answer to, "Should I write about X?" will be, "It depends on how you write about it." And the rest of this section covers how to write about any challenge.

2. How much sharing is too much?

Generally speaking, we don't need to know all the details of the challenges you faced. In other words, we don't need, "My father punched me in the face, breaking my nose and sending blood spurting all over the kitchen floor. I watched the blood as it oozed between the cracks in the blue-and-white linoleum tiles..." We just need enough information to get a sense of what you experienced. So, in this case, it would be enough to say, "There were even times when my father was physically abusive."

As a general rule, you don't need to shock the reader to make your point.

Column 2: Effects

What negative effects did you experience as a result of the challenges you faced? (Note that you probably experienced some positive effects, too, but save those for the column 4, which is labeled "values.")

The purpose of this section is to differentiate <u>your</u> experiences from those of <u>everyone else</u> who went through (and is writing his or her college essay about) similar challenges.

For example, Student A and Student B may have both experienced the challenge of "bullying," but Student A might list "physical abuse," and "having to switch schools" in the "Effects" column, whereas Student B might list "ridicule" and "name-calling."

Or two students may have the same medical condition, but for one student that may have meant trips to the allergy specialist for several years (see the "Porcelain God" essay on page 54), while for another student that may have meant a week away from school (see the "Bowling" essay on page 85). And there's no better or worse here; the point is that by providing more information, you differentiate your experiences from those of others.

Two important things to remember as you're brainstorming this section:

1. You don't need precisely one effect per challenge—one challenge can have several repercussions.
2. This part can take some time, so be patient.

Column 3: What I Did

What actions did you take to improve your situation?

Examples: I started watching the parenting videos our family counselor had given my dad, I took a train from London to Paris, or I created two organizations to improve sustainability on campus.

Column 4: Values

What qualities/skills/values/resources did you develop during this time?

Here's an example based on the brainstorm for the "Bowling" essay on page 85:

1. Challenges	2. Effects	3. What I Did	4. Values
father's accident	Cup of Noodles soup	connected w/ mom more	family, sacrifice
baby sister car accident	I missed school to work	Leadership Council	confidence
mother's tumor	hurt myself (vein lea.k.a.ge)	GSA (anti-bullying)	self-love
		soccer (captain)	leadership
		job (bowling alley)	fun

IMPORTANT NOTE: See if you can include several *unexpected* connections or values. Let me explain. Some of the connections between the "what I did" and the "values" are pretty obvious. But a few of them are less obvious, such as the connections between "GSA (anti-bullying)" and "self-love" or between "connected with mom more" and "sacrifice." It's these unusual values—or usual values developed in unusual ways—that can lead to unique insights and make your essay stand out.

And the point I just made is so important that I feel I must underscore it:

If you use only predictable values at the end of your essay and explain your values in predictable ways, there is a good chance your essay will be boring.

- Examples of predictable values gained from being the captain of the soccer team: discipline, commitment, hard work
- Examples of unpredictable values gained from being the captain of the soccer team: emotional risk, autonomy, healthy boundaries

Which group of values might make for a more interesting essay? That's a rhetorical question, but just in case: the second group. Just to get your brain turning, here's one more set of examples:

- Predictable values gained from joining Model United Nations: responsibility, sacrifice, helping others
- Unpredictable values gained from joining Model United Nations: resourcefulness, art, privacy

IMPORTANT NOTE: Just because the values are predictable doesn't mean that they are wrong or boring or that you are wrong or boring. I've read great essays that have used predictable values, but here's the key: the more usual the values are, the more well-crafted (or unusual) the "so what" moments need to be. Notice, for example, that the "Bowling" essay on page 85 includes the theme of "hard work," which could be considered a predictable value—that's fine, and the essay still works. I'm simply suggesting you either include a couple unusual values or express your predictable values in an interesting (or at least succinct) way.

HOW CAN YOU BRAINSTORM LESS PREDICTABLE VALUES?

Try this: look at the Core Values Exercise on page 8 and see if you can choose a value you think will surprise me. (Yes, me, Ethan.) Imagine we're actually sitting across from each other and you've just told me about your challenge and what you did about it. Then pick a value on that list and imagine telling me what you gained from it. If you think I'll be able to guess the connection, chances are it'll be predictable for the reader. So pick something else. Keep going until you find something that you don't think I'd be able to guess right away.

STEP 2: DECIDE ON A STRUCTURE.

Here's a simple structure for organizing your essay:

1. What's the challenge I faced? (≈ 1/3 of essay; it could be a bit more, but not more than 1/2! The essay should turn from negative "challenges" to positive "what I did" by the midway point.)
2. What did I do about it? (≈ 1/3 of essay)
3. How did this make me a better person? (≈ 1/3 of essay)

So, if you're writing a 650-word essay, the math works out like this:

1. Challenge(s): ≈ 150–250 words
2. What I did: ≈ 150–250 words
3. What I learned: ≈ 150–250 words

This is just a guide. It's totally possible to break from this form and still write a great essay, but this is a good starting point to keep you on track.

Two Common Pitfalls When Discussing Challenges in an Essay (and How to Avoid Them)

1. Avoid articulating the "challenge" and the "what I did" in the same sentence, like this:

My mother injured her back, so I had to take on more responsibility around the house by cleaning the house and cooking meals for my brothers.

This ruins the ending of the story. Why? I'll explain in a second.

2. Avoid jumping back and forth between the "challenge" and "what I did" several times in the same paragraph, like this:

My mother hurt her back, so I started helping more around the house, I started falling behind in school, so I taught myself to manage my time better, and responsibilities as soccer captain increased, so I learned to delegate responsibilities better.

This creates two problems:

1. It can ruin the ending (thanks, that's the whole essay, goodbye!).
2. It can lead to an essay that feels disorganized.

How do you solve this?

Group all the challenges into one paragraph and don't solve the problems until later in the essay, in a separate paragraph.

Why should you do this?

1. Grouping all the challenges into an early paragraph allows time for the reader to wonder, "Are things going to work out? If so, how?" It builds tension.

2. It organizes the information in a way that allows you to have a
   narrative arc that looks something like this:

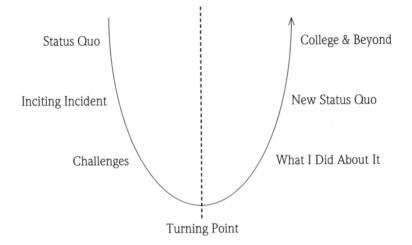

Status Quo   College & Beyond

Inciting Incident   New Status Quo

Challenges   What I Did About It

Turning Point

You'll notice this follows the narrative structure. That's the idea.
To review:

- **Status Quo**: how things were at one point
- **Inciting Incident**: the moment the changes began
- **Raise the Stakes**: the tough stuff
- **Turning Point/Moment of Truth**: the moment you decided
  to do something about it
- **Denouement/What I Did**: describe in detail the specific
  actions you took
- **New Status Quo**: what changed, or how things are now

Interesting note: The "Raising Anthony" essay on page 26 does
not follow this structure precisely. In fact, its arc looks more like this:

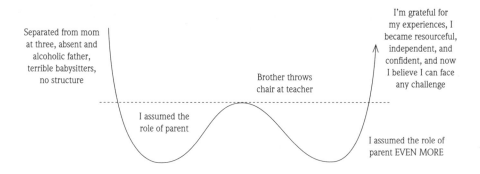

Why this structure? Because otherwise it's too easy to spend most of the essay describing the "challenges" and not enough time describing "what I did" or "what I learned"—which is what admissions officers are most interested in knowing.

Want an even more specific outline? I'll give you one in just a second, and I'll even include some paragraph starters to give you a sense of how the essay might flow. But remember this: don't use this sample outline if it feels too confining. Use it only if you're feeling lost or if you really need a more specific structure. With those qualifiers, here is:

A PAINT-BY-NUMBER OUTLINE FOR A TYPE C ESSAY

1. THE CHALLENGES (OR) THE EFFECTS: ≈ 1/3 OF ESSAY (AND NO MORE THAN 1/2!)

❏ **Paragraph 1**: My life was forever changed when…
❏ **Paragraph 2**: To make matters worse…
   ❏ Transition sentences (the lowest point of the story):
      ❏ Sentence 1 (the breaking point): The toughest part came when…
      ❏ Sentence 2 (the turning point): I realized I had to do something.

2. WHAT I DID (OR) THE WORK I PUT IN: ≈ 1/3 OF ESSAY

☐ **Paragraph 3**: So I started… (Describe the specific things you did to make things better.)

☐ **Paragraph 4**: I also… (What else did you do? Describe the specifics here.)

> **Tip for increasing the drama:** In these two paragraphs, build the details from smallest to largest.
>
> Example: "I started helping my brother with his homework" should come before "I founded an environmental science club at my school and began holding weekly meetings," since presumably the homework help required less work than founding a club and holding weekly meetings.

> **Tip for the transition between paragraphs 4 and 5:** In order to clearly demonstrate that things have improved, create a "stand up and cheer" moment at the end of paragraph 4 that involves one specific detail or image that shows you at your best.
>
> Example: "And to top it all off, I got straight As for the first time ever" or "Then I did something with my brother that I hadn't done in six years: I ate dinner with him." This moment represents an opportunity to show how far you've come. (See the "Bowling" or "I Shot My Brother" essay for an example.)

3. WHAT I LEARNED (OR) THE RESULT: ≈ 1/3 OF ESSAY

☐ **Paragraph 5**: Turn your difficulties into strengths.

Example 1: Having to balance schoolwork, plus chores, plus a job, taught me the value of time management.

Example 2: Overcommitting myself with four AP classes, six clubs, and two jobs taught me how important it is to prioritize and how to say "no."

WHAT NOW?

Time to outline and write a draft using the instructions in this section. You can use any of the following:

- The simple three-part outline (Challenges, What I did, What I learned) described on page 80
- The narrative structure described on page 82
- The paint-by-number outline for a type C essay on page 83
- The Feelings and Needs Exercise on page 127 (if you really want to take your essay to the next level)

Once you've written a draft, turn to "How to Revise Your Essay in Five Steps" on page 102.

Want two more examples of type C essays?

Here you go:

"BOWLING"

*Written by a student who did **face significant challenges** and **did** not know **what she wanted to study***

Every weekend, my family and I go to the bowling alley. We either go to Lucky Strike in Orange County, to 300 in Pasadena or the AMF Bowladrome in Torrance. It's been a tradition for us ever since I turned 11. But here's a secret:

I've never bowled a game in my life.

I began going when I was 11 because that's when I was old enough to adroitly wipe down a table and spray Windex on a window without making a mess. Every Saturday night from 10pm to 4am, after entering the bowling alley through a back door, my parents dispatch my older sister Marlene and me to the lanes armed with broomsticks.

"Try to clean around the bowlers," she always says.

We always do.

In 2003 my family's stability was put to the test when my father suffered an accident: he was bitten by a horse and unable to work for three years. Some months later my year-old baby sister was hit by a car. My mother was our only financial support, so we often ate Cup of Noodles for breakfast, lunch and dinner. I prayed every night that things got [sic] better but first they got worse.

In the eleventh grade my father suffered a muscle failure and my mother was diagnosed with a tumor. Due to my parents' health problems I took on more responsibilities, sometimes missing school to care for my younger sisters and helping my father and mother at their work. Unfortunately, I pushed myself so hard that I ended up hurting myself, suffering a vain [sic] lea.k.a.ge in my brain. I was the fighter, the protector, and now I found myself needing someone to protect me. I was glad to have my mother by my side because she gave the strength I needed.

After some rest, I returned to school more focused than ever on preparing for my future. I got involved in Leadership Council where I'm now part of the civics committee, planning events such as Day at the Park and school dances. I've also become a big supporter of the Gay Straight Alliance that deals with anti-bullying, and through this club I've given presentations that address unfairness and promote equity. But perhaps my biggest support system has come through the four years on my high school soccer team, where my commitment and love for soccer won me the captain position for the past two years.

I know I'm not like many students my age, but I'm happy with who I am. I am the student who works on the weekends scrubbing restrooms, carrying trash bags and mopping kitchen floors. I am the student who won't give a second thought to missing a party to help my parents babysit my sisters or accompany them to a new job. I know that one day I will not take my family to a bowling alley to clean it but to enjoy it. And who knows, maybe one day I will learn to bowl.

Note that this essay follows the recommended structure, but with a slight variation: rather than describing the "challenge," "what [she] did," and "what [she] learned" in one-third chunks, the author instead dedicates the first one-fourth of the essay to setting up a hook, then devotes one-fourth to each of the other parts. This is fine and good. Again, the suggested structure is just a guide to get you to communicate the challenges succinctly so you can focus on other elements in the essay.

"WHAT I FOUND ON THE FARM"
Written by a student who did *face significant challenges* and did not know *what he wanted to study*

"In the first six years of my life, my family moved exactly thirteen times. By the fifth move, the security of 'home' was gone. By the ninth, my eyes had adjusted to the aggressive two-dimensionality of the Affordable Housing Authority's drab brick walls. This was my life: only drifting, transience. No roots, no permanence."

My voice trembled beneath the dim dining hall lights as I sat before sixty students and two dozen faculty members. I shared my world as a first-generation Asian-American, how my mother's first job in America had been a seamstress in an overstuffed Chinese garment factory, and how my grandmother, in her seventies, spent her last years in the Land of Opportunity scavenging cans on city streets.

Here I was, three hundred miles from home in the Colorado backcountry, opening my heart to strangers. Why?

For the past few years, I'd found myself the bearer of rather peculiar labels from my peers, creative terms like "banana" and "golden Oreo." Perhaps it was because my Chinese language ability (or lack thereof) was my family's shame, or because I absolutely could not use chopsticks for the life of me. Maybe it was because even though I tried and tried, I could not play Pachelbel's Canon in D. Whatever it was, I was accused of letting my "Chinese-ness" slip. I was stuck in limbo, truly belonging to neither the Chinese nor the American community. I felt closed-off and lost.

I yearned for a place to belong. But where? In my junior year, I found it—in Colorado, of all places.

At the Colorado Ranch School, a summer program on a farm in rural Colorado, I bucked my home culture of over-scheduling and over-stimulation. Living together with my teachers and their children, witnessing one too many animal slaughters with my classmates, and harvesting all 2,000 pounds of sweet potatoes until our nails caked with dried dirt, I felt comfortable enough, for the very first time, to share my deepest stories.

I also discovered a refreshing approach to activism, one that valued student voices, respected individualism, and championed student-led change—values not as esteemed at my home school. When the issue of racial microaggressions emerged, for example, I created an affinity group to increase awareness about diversity issues, holding conversations that unified students and staff to effect change in our school.

But most importantly, I found a place where I belonged, and with it, a sense of community and acceptance.

In the spring, I returned to high school refreshed and empowered. I created two organizations to improve sustainability on campus, fundraising thousands to install water stations to reduce plastic bottle consumption. Realizing the value of fighting for change, I protested outside the White House at the Keystone XL Dissent rally and marched alongside a legion of 400,000 at the People's Climate March, demanding action to save our planet.

Before the Colorado Ranch School, I let others define me, based on the titles they chose to bestow upon me: "banana," "golden Oreo," even tree-hugger. But in Colorado, despite the rootlessness and transience of my upbringing, I was able to solidify a strengthened sense of self: environmentalist, activist, Asian-American. By showing my authentic self to a group of compassionate individuals, I realized that I'm so much more than those confining titles: I'm the son of hardworking immigrant parents, the lover of anything by Junot Diaz, the one for whom mixing cereal and milk is a personal sin.

Chopsticks still fluster me, and I can't magically play Pachelbel, but so be it. My identity is just that: mine to own, and mine to shape. In time, I've learned that while my identity already has, and will continue to change, I can embrace it for what it is: a medley of unorthodox traits, passions, and dreams, blending into a singular vibrant whole.

Note that this essay basically uses the one-third, one-third, one-third structure suggested earlier, as the "challenge," "what I did," and "what I learned" sections are all about the same length. Also note that the author begins the essay not with his inciting incident, but with the turning point—in other words, he starts with the moment that he was able to find what he was looking for—a community where he could feel safe enough to be vulnerable. This works great.

HOW TO WRITE ESSAY TYPE D

For Students Who *Have Not* Faced Significant Challenges and *Do Not Know* What They Want to Study

If you haven't experienced significant challenges and aren't sure what you'd like to study, you may be wondering what to write about. Don't worry. You'll be generating ideas in a few minutes.

Consider that in broad terms you're looking for:

1. **Content**: some stuff (values or qualities) that you want to discuss
2. **Structure**: a way to frame all the stuff—an angle, a focusing lens

How do you find a great focusing lens? We'll get to that in a second. But first, I want to emphasize something.

The Importance of Being Patient

Type D essays are the most open-ended of the four types. Think for a second about why that may be.

Type A and C essays dedicate a lot of their word count to describing the author's challenges and efforts to overcome them, while type B essays are dedicated to describing values that will serve the author in a particular career.

But for type D essays, nothing is set. It's wide open. What does this mean for you?

You'll need to be patient.

It's very possible to write an interesting essay that has no major conflict and mentions no definitive career choice in its conclusion. (You'll find examples on pages 28, 96, 99, 152, and 207.) Because your options are wide open, it just might take you a little longer. How much longer? As a reference point, the type D essays mentioned above took at least eight to ten drafts to complete.

THE SECRET TO WRITING THIS TYPE OF ESSAY

Find a focusing lens that allows you to discuss a wide range of values or qualities.

The type D essays in this book (see list on page 231) all utilize a framing device that allowed their authors to demonstrate a variety of values. In the "Scrapbook" essay on page 28, for example, the author was able to bring to life the values of travel, teaching, family, and helping others through the "scrapbook of [her] life." In the "Five Families" essay on page 152, the author describes how living in five different homes helped him learn the importance of humility, intimacy, openness, discipline, diversity, and adaptability.

How did these authors do this? First, they generated some stuff to write about, and then they figured out a way to organize all their stuff. Did they have to start over several times? Yes. Did they get frustrated along the way? Definitely. But both authors worked hard, they didn't give up, and ultimately they wrote great essays.

It's your turn. First, you need your content, so here are:

SIX WAYS TO GENERATE YOUR CONTENT (A.K.A. SOME STUFF YOU WANT THE READER TO KNOW ABOUT YOU)

Complete the following exercises:

1. Essence Objects Exercise (page 1)
2. Core Values Exercise (page 8)
3. 21 Details Exercise (page 225)
4. Everything I Want Colleges to Know about Me List (page 226)

5. Time Line of My Life Exercise (page 228), either alone or with someone else
6. Complete a personality assessment online (many are available and some are free).

Once you've finished these exercises, most of which should take between five and twenty minutes, you should have several (or many) gems—qualities or values that you definitely want to communicate in your essay. If not, keep going—you may have rushed through the process.

Once you've completed the exercises, look for a way to organize your content—in other words, a structure. Here are:

SIX WAYS TO IDENTIFY A FRAMING DEVICE FOR YOUR ESSAY

Remember: A great framing device (i.e., focusing lens) is one that allows you to discuss a wide variety of values. Here are some ideas.

Option 1: Use a placeholder career and discuss values essential to that career (i.e., write a type B essay).
That's right—before we even get into the type D tips—ask yourself if you could actually write a type B essay using a placeholder.

What's a placeholder career? It means picking something you're interested in and mentioning it as a potential future career at the end of your essay. Say, for example, you love math, you're interested in studying business, and you love helping others—you might say at the end of your essay that you're interested in being a "socially conscious entrepreneur."

Fun Fact: Some of the essays in this book actually have career placeholders. But I'm not going to tell you which ones, and *you'll never be able to guess them.*

And, by the way, isn't *every* career a placeholder in the long run?

Here are two benefits to this method:

1. **A placeholder can actually help you find your calling**. It's true. I once worked with a student who wasn't sure what she wanted to study, but she knew she was interested in travel, working with people, and global issues. So she chose a travel-related major (international relations) as a placeholder and was able to write an essay describing how her interests and family background led her to become interested in this field. And guess what? By researching international relations, she actually ended up becoming more interested in it, and it went from being a placeholder to a college major that she was excited about. Will choosing a placeholder always lead you to find your calling? Not always. But it might.

2. **Focusing on how you developed a core set of values might also save you time**. I recently worked with a student who thought he wanted to major in computer science, so we started brainstorming an essay by naming some of the values that had led him to that field: autonomy, creativity, and helping others. A few weeks before his essay was due, however, he decided he was interested in studying psychology and potentially becoming a counselor. Fortunately, he didn't have to start his essay over from scratch. Why? We'd been focusing on core values that connected to many majors, so he was able to salvage a good portion of his essay. How? Because while computer scientists value autonomy, creativity, and helping others, so do counselors. So he was able to keep most of his essay, which detailed how he'd developed these values. He simply rewrote the ending, explaining what these values all added up to. Just to clarify: this will work as long as the values you've been focusing on in your essay will connect to your new career path—and, by the way, most values will connect to most careers.

My main point here is this: Because I believe that, ultimately, every career is a placeholder, what's most important is not where we end up, but how we get there. Put another way, admissions officers are less interested in what you want to be (career) and more interested in how you arrived there (values). In short, prioritize process over product, journey over destination.

What's the best way to discover a potential major or career? I use the book *Do What You Are*, by Paul D. Tieger, Barbara Barron, and Kelly Tieger, which provides profiles for different careers based on a student's personality.

If you would rather not write about a potential career or major, here are some other ways to find a focusing lens.

Option 2: Search for common themes among your brainstorm exercises.

Ask yourself: Do any themes repeat in my brainstorming material?

Example: *I'm noticing the theme of "home" coming up a lot. What does "home" really mean to me? Could I write an essay exploring my relationship to home, and how the meaning of "home" has shifted for me throughout my life?*

Another example: *I'm noticing the theme of "being a man" has come up a few times. What does it mean to me to "be a man" and how has my thinking on that evolved over the years?*

Option 3: Look for interesting contradictions.

Ask yourself: Do I spot any interesting opposites, contradictions, or paradoxes in my brainstorming material?

Example from a past student: *Some of my essence objects demonstrate my passion for collaboration, while a few of my 21 details mention how much I love working by myself. What does this say about me? Could I write an essay exploring these two parts of myself—my desire for both autonomy and connectedness?*

Another example from a past student: *Some of my essence objects represent my connection to Korean culture, while other details represent my connection to American culture. How do I feel about this? Am I torn between the two, connected to them equally, or both?* (Apologies to you, dear reader, that I can't include all these essays—this book would be crazy long. But many are available on the College Essay Guy website: www.collegeessayguy.com.)

Option 4: Look for a potential negative and turn it into a positive.

Ask yourself: Is there a potential red flag on my application? Anything the reader might question? How could I reframe this so that it might actually be seen as a strength?

Example from a past student: *I feel like I'm all over the place with my extracurricular activities. What positive quality could all this jumping around represent? Ooh! How about an ability to adapt to all sorts of scenarios—like a chameleon?* (Careful here: make sure your essay doesn't sound like an elaborate excuse. How will you do this? Over the course of several drafts, my friend.)

Option 5: List your top three (or five) life lessons.

Ask yourself: What three to five moments, events, or lessons really shaped who I am?

Example from an essay in this book: *Some people see me as "the debate guy" or "the writer" or even the guy who got a great SAT score. But that's not really me—I'm more of a punk rock philosopher. Could I write about how I became that?* (Yes. See the "Punk Rock Philosopher" essay that on page 96.)

Option 6: Choose something that you love and write about it unabashedly.

Is there anything in your life that you love to do that could serve as a focusing lens?

Example from a past student: *I love beekeeping. Seriously, it's like my favorite thing. It's helped me connect with my dad, it's taught me about nature, and even about business, since I've started selling the honey that our bees have produced. Could I write an essay on The Top Five Lessons I've Learned from Beekeeping?* (Um, yes. Absolutely.)

Another example: *I love reading. Could my essay be all about how books have shaped me?* Yes—see the "If Ink Were Ants" essay on page 99.

Ready for some examples of essays built from these options? You'll find two here and others by searching the index at the back of the book.

"PUNK ROCK PHILOSOPHER"
Written by a student who did not *face significant challenges and* did not know *what he wanted to study*

I am on Oxford Academy's Speech and Debate Team, in both the Parliamentary Debate division and the Lincoln-Douglass debate division. I write screenplays, short stories, and opinionated blogs and am a regular contributor to my school literary magazine, *The Gluestick.* I have accumulated over 300 community service hours that includes work at homeless shelters, libraries, and special education youth camps. I have been evaluated by the College Board and have placed within the top percentile.

But I am not any of these things. I am not a test score, nor a debater, nor a writer. I am an anti-nihilist punk rock philosopher. And I became so when I realized three things:

1) That the world is ruled by underwear. There is a variety of underwear for a variety of people. You have your ironed briefs for your businessmen, your soft cottons for the average, and hemp-based underwear for your environmental romantics. But underwear do [sic] not only tell us about who we are, they [sic] also influence our daily interactions in ways most of us don't even understand. For example, I have a specific pair of underwear that is holey, worn out but surprisingly comfortable. And despite how trivial underwear might be, when I am wearing my

favorite pair, I feel as if I am on top of the world. In any case, these articles of clothing affect our being and are the unsung heroes of comfort.

2) When I realized I cannot understand the world. I recently debated at the Orange County Speech League Tournament, within the Parliamentary Division. This specific branch of debate is an hour long, and consists of two parties debating either side of a current political issue. In one particular debate, I was assigned the topic: "Should Nation States eliminate nuclear arms?" It so happened that I was on the negative side and it was my job to convince the judges that countries should continue manufacturing nuclear weapons. During the debate, something strange happened: I realized that we are a special breed of species, that so much effort and resources are invested to ensure mutual destruction. And I felt that this debate in a small college classroom had elucidated something much more profound about the scale of human existence. In any case, I won 1st place at the tournament, but as the crowd cheered when my name was called to stand before an audience of hundreds of other debaters, and I flashed a victorious smile at the cameras, I couldn't help but imagine that somewhere at that moment a nuclear bomb was being manufactured, adding to an ever-growing stockpile of doom. And that's when I realized that the world was something I will never understand.

3) When I realized I was a punk rocker philosopher. One summer night, my friend took me to an underground hardcore punk rock show. It was inside a small abandoned church. After the show, I met and became a part of this small community. Many were lost and on a constant soul-search, and to my surprise, many, like myself, did not have a blue Mohawk or a nose piercing. Many were just ordinary people discussing Nietzsche, string theory, and governmental ideologies. Many were also artists creating promotional posters and inventive

slogans for stickers. They were all people my age who could not afford to be part of a record label and did something extraordinary by playing in these abandoned churches, making their own CDs and making thousands of promotional buttons by hand. I realized then that punk rock is not about music nor is it a guy with a blue Mohawk screaming protests. Punk rock is an attitude, a mindset, and very much a culture. It is an antagonist to the conventional. It means making the best with what you have to contribute to a community. This was when I realized that I was a punk rock philosopher.

The world I come from consists of underwear, nuclear bombs, and punk rockers. And I love this world. My world is inherently complex, mysterious, and anti-nihilist. I am Daniel Bak, somebody who spends his weekends debating in a three-piece suit, other days immersed within the punk rock culture, and some days writing opinionated blogs about underwear.

But why college? I want a higher education. I want more than just the textbook fed classrooms in high school. A community which prizes revolutionary ideals, a sharing of multi-dynamical perspectives, an environment that ultimately acts as a medium for movement, similar to the punk rock community. I do not see college as a mere stepping stone for a stable career or a prosperous life, but as a supplement for knowledge and self-empowerment; it is a social engine that will jettison us to our next paradigm shift.

Note the simple framing device. The author names all his achievements and then undercuts them by writing, "But I am not any of these things. I am not a test score, nor a debater, nor a writer. I am an anti-nihilist punk rock philosopher. And I became so when I realized three things…" and just like that, I'm hooked. I totally want to know what those three things are. He does so by raising a question that's interesting enough to keep our attention for the length of the essay (something that's discussed more on page 112). In this case, the question is simple: What were the three lessons the author learned that led him to become an anti-nihilist punk rock philosopher?

"IF INK WERE ANTS"

Written by a student who did not *face significant challenges and* did not know *what she wanted to study*

"If the ink of my writing morphed into ants, would they march along with my thoughts?" ~ *Jarod Kintz*

Wooden bookshelves protrude regally from my wall. The wall's deep purple stucco contrasts starkly with the boards' glossy white granules. Atop the shelves, several volumes rise in lofty columns. The columns tremble. A strange commotion ripples through their pages.

Sprawled upon one such page, I feel the parchment beneath me shuddering like the earth beneath a wild stampede. Before my incredulous eyes, the typed letters before me quiver, totter... morph into ants! The ants march to and fro across the page, ravenously following thoughts of quarks, hidden dimensions, and string theory. I am in Brian Greene's scientific novel, *The Elegant Universe.* I want to join the ants and delve into the author's thoughts. Instead, I reflect on my memories:

Awe overwhelmed my middle-school mind. My hand, a bottle cap, everything, was composed of not only atoms, but of smaller quarks, which were not static points, but oscillating strings. Everything in my life might be controlled by infinitesimal, interconnected loops... the universe, a mind-bogglingly large space, might be only one of an infinite number of universes. After studying cosmology at an extra-curricular astro-camp, I was certain: I wanted to be a theoretical physicist.

I haul myself out of Greene's novel and observe a stream of ants spilling from *Pride and Prejudice, Gone with the Wind,* and *Crime and Punishment.* I join their ranks, revisiting scenes of ballrooms, Civil War battles, 19th century St. Petersburg. Again, my thoughts wander:

As a sophomore, I loved venturing into the worlds of historic characters. AP European History quickly became my favorite class. I obsessed with particulars: Queen Elizabeth I and her rumored romantic interest in Sir Walter Raleigh, the infamous schemes and bizarre execution of the Russian monk, Rasputin. Studying history was like reading a novel, and I was determined to uncover the plots. I aspired to become an historian.

As we vacate *Crime and Punishment,* the ant before me halts jarringly. I pitch forward precariously. My arms whirl in a windmill-like motion. I plunge over the ant's back into another novel.

An ant nudges me from the left. Another from the right. All around me, the ants career spasmodically—here, there, everywhere! As I listen to the thoughts swirling about I deduce the cause of the chaos: the little creatures cannot decipher my Latin copy of *Carmina.*

I remembered translating Catullus' poetry, analyzing his dysfunctional relationship with Lesbia. Wishing to grasp Catullus' motivations and thought processes, I realized that it would be fascinating to study psychology.

I squeeze beneath *Carmina*'s cover and spot my ceramic teddy-bear bookend looming above me. Struck by a sudden impulse, I scale its towering form and settle comfortably between the figurine's ears, my legs dangling over its eyes, and survey my bedroom. Around me, my books pitch and heave mightily as ants swell from their covers. A black sea of scuttling limbs, the ants pour out of *Atlas Shrugged, A Long Way Gone, Star Trek, Harry Potter,* and Dickens novels, and dozens more. They surge toward the center of my room, billow beneath my bed, and... disappear. The boisterous, animate rabble of thoughts vanishes, leaving behind the whisper of empty pages rustling blankly.

I withdraw from my daydream and scrutinize my college application. The old, but now more pressing, question batters my brain: "What do you want to be when you grow up?" I contemplate my bookshelves and the stories that have shaped my identity and aspirations and am struck by the power of ink on paper to persuade, inform, and inspire. I select the English option from the application menu. My future might be undecided but surely pursuing my passionate interest in literature is the best way to fill its pages. I eye my copy of *One L.* *Perhaps an English degree will lead to a J.D. in law...*

Again, note the simple framing device. The author seems to say, *Here are a few ways that books have shaped my interests.* Straightforward enough. But the way the author tells of their influence is unusual, unexpected, and beautifully crafted. In fact, note that the insights and craft in both this essay and the "Punk Rock Philosopher" essay are on another level. I believe that for an essay that does not address a particular challenge to really stand out, careful attention must be paid to the insights (or "so what" moments) and the craft (*how* the story is told). To be sure, these elements are always important, but I think they are especially important when writing the type D essay. As I've mentioned, it can sometimes take longer to find an unusual framing device and to craft the insights, but it is possible with some hard work and patience. As a point of reference, the author of the "If Ink Were Ants" essay and I had a conversation about an entirely different essay, which she ultimately decided to scrap after our conversation. Several weeks later, after not hearing from her, she wrote me an email that read, "I finally finished the new draft of my essay (after 10 revisions!)" and she attached the essay you just read. Because, sometimes, that's what it takes.

How to Revise Your Essay in Five Steps

REVISING THE FIRST DRAFT

Some of the essays you've read so far have a structure that is rock solid. Not only is it rock solid, it's one we can learn from.

Take a look at the first sentence of each paragraph from type A essay "With Debate" (page 22) and type B essay "Endodontics" (page 24).

Notice something?

If you read just those sentences, each essay still makes sense. They're like mini-essays. Take a look:

Here's the first line of each paragraph of the "With Debate" essay:

The clock was remarkably slow as I sat, legs tightly crossed, squirming at my desk.

My diffidence was frustrating.

Near meltdown, I knew something needed to be done.

Disillusioned and wrung dry of ideas, I followed my mom's advice and joined a debate club.

But soon, the club moved on from "how to make a speech" lessons to the exploration of argumentation.

By high school, I joined the school debate team, began socializing, and was even elected to head several clubs.

I became proud and confident.

Four years with debate, and now I'm the kid up at the white board; the kid leading discussions; and the kid standing up for her beliefs.

More importantly, I now confront issues instead of avoiding them.

In particular, I am interested in the North-South Korean tension.

I see a reflection of myself in the divide at the 38th parallel because I see one part isolating itself in defense to outside threats, and another part coming out to face the world as one of the fastest-developing nations.

And here's the first line of each paragraph of the "Endodontics" essay:

As a kid I was always curious.

And it didn't stop in second grade.

A few years later I designed my first pair of shoes, working for hours to perfect each detail, including whether the laces should be mineral white or diamond white.

In high school I moved on to more advanced projects, teaching myself how to take apart, repair, and customize cell phones.

And once I obtained my driver's license, I began working on cars.

My love of details applies to my schoolwork too.

I'm the math geek who marvels at the fundamental theorems of Calculus, or who sees beauty in $A = (s(s-a)(s-b)(s-c))^{\wedge}(1/2)$.

I also love sharing this appreciation with others and have taken it upon myself to personally eradicate mathonumopho-biconfundosis, my Calculus teacher's term for "extreme fear of Math."

You probably think I want to be a designer. Or perhaps an engineer?

Wrong. Well, kind of.

Actually, I want to study Endodontics, which is (I'll save you the Wikipedia look-up) a branch of dentistry that deals with the tooth pulp and the tissues surrounding the root of a tooth.

The fact is, it's not unlike the work I've been doing repairing cellphone circuits and modifying cars, though there is one small difference.

The question is: Will the toothbrushes I hand out be mineral white or diamond white?

Kind of awesome. Almost as if the whole essay could be boiled down to those first sentences.

How can this help you revise your essay? Like this:

1. Go through your essay and highlight the first sentence of each

paragraph in bold. Then read the bolded lines aloud. (Side note: I once heard that Anton Chekhov would read all his work aloud to his wife to check for sense and errors—it's a great practice. Even if you have no wife.)

As you read, you'll probably notice that some parts make sense and some parts don't.

So:

2. Write a new outline in which all of the first sentences flow together like a mini-version of your essay.
3. Once you've written this new outline, paste the bolded lines onto a brand new blank document.

Then:

4. Rewrite your paragraphs so that each paragraph fleshes out the topic sentence.

This may not sound like a very romantic or creative way of writing an essay, but it works. It'll also help you clarify what you're trying to say. "Foggy writing is foggy thinking," my favorite English teacher, Mrs. Clark, used to say.

Why do I suggest you paste the new outline onto a new document and start over? Because, in short, it'll take longer if you don't. Chances are you'll have fallen in love with your first way of phrasing something. Once you've written the new outline, though, that old phrasing dies. And if you're trying to create a new and living thing out of old, dead parts, you're no better than Dr. Frankenstein. And we all know what happened to him.

5. Step away from the essay for at least thirty minutes. Go for a walk, get something to eat, do something else to clear your mind.

Then come back to the essay and read it aloud. When you do:

- Highlight the first sentence of each paragraph in bold.
- Read the bolded sentences aloud in order to see if they now tell a short version of your essay. (If not, rewrite them.) If they do...
- Read the whole essay aloud, checking to see if what's in each paragraph supports the sentences in bold.

If they do, you should have a very solid revision, maybe even one that's ready for feedback.

REVISING DRAFTS 2–50

What if you've just done the first sentence revision exercise and your essay still doesn't flow? Make sure you've tried it a couple times or even had someone else guide you through it—sometimes an outside eye can help. Also make sure this person has read the description of this exercise, so he or she understands what you're trying to do here.

Still isn't working? It may be that your problem isn't the "flow" of your ideas at all. It may actually be that your essay doesn't reveal much about you or that it's not that deep.

If you suspect that one of these things is the case, turn to page 186 and read "The Great College Essay Test" or to page 121 to learn how to make your essay, like, deep.

CHAPTER SIX

How to Bring Your Essay to Life

(or) How to Make It Not Boring

HERE ARE SOME QUESTIONS I get a lot:

- How do I grab the reader's attention?
- How do I show the reader that I'm really smart?
- How do I brag in a way that doesn't sound like I'm bragging?
- How do I make my essay, like, deep?
- How do I end my essay?

And here are my thoughts on these matters.

HOW DO I GRAB THE READER'S ATTENTION?

Your English teacher has probably told you, "Your essay needs a hook!" or "You've gotta draw 'em in!"

Thanks. The question is: How?

Here's my favorite way:

Begin with a Problem That Must Be Solved

Examples:

"Porcelain God" (page 54)

Bowing down to the porcelain god, I emptied the contents of my stomach. Foaming at the mouth, I was ready to pass out. My body couldn't stop shaking as I gasped for air, and the room started spinning.

Problem: What happened? Why is she throwing up? Will she be okay? Will she die?

"I Shot My Brother" (page 173)

From page 54 of the maroon notebook sitting on my mahogany desk:
Then Cain said to the Lord, "My punishment is greater than I can bear. I shall be a fugitive and a wanderer on the earth and whoever finds me will kill me."—Genesis 4:13
Here is a secret that no one in my family knows: I shot my brother when I was six. Luckily, it was a BB gun. But to this day, my older brother Jonathan does not know who shot him. And I have finally promised myself to confess this eleven year old secret to him after I write this essay.

Problem: Why did he shoot his brother? How? Will he actually get up the nerve to confess? How will his brother react?

"Rock, Paper, Scissors" (page 169)

Prompt:
Dear Christian, The admissions staff at the University of

Chicago would like to inform you that your application has been "put on the line." We have one spot left and can't decide if we should admit you or another equally qualified applicant. To resolve the matter, please choose one of the following:

Rock, paper, or scissors.

You will be notified of our decision shortly.

Response:

Rock beats scissors, scissors beats paper, and paper beats rock. Wait... paper beats rock? Since when has a sheet of loose leaf paper ever defeated a solid block of granite? Do we assume that the paper wraps around the rock, smothering the rock into submission? When exposed to paper, is rock somehow immobilized, unable to fulfill its primary function of smashing scissors? What constitutes defeat between two inanimate objects?

Problem: Which will he choose? How will he decide? What if he makes the wrong choice?

IMPORTANT NOTE: Don't solve the problem until the end of the essay. OR: If you choose to solve the problem or answer the question partway through the essay, make sure you create a new problem or ask a new question that won't be answered until the end. In the "I Shot My Brother" essay, for example, the author answers the question of *how* he shot him (with a BB gun) in the first paragraph. But he doesn't answer *why* he shot him until later in the essay, and (advanced technique) he never tells us in the essay how his brother reacted to finding out who shot him, something that gives the essay an elliptical ending. (See "Four Qualities of an Amazing Essay" on page 178 for more on this.)

Variation: Start with an Image That Doesn't Make Any Sense

It can also be effective to begin with something that makes the reader wonder, "How in the world is this relevant for a college admissions essay?"

Examples:

"Dying Bird" (page 176)

Smeared blood, shredded feathers. Clearly, the bird was dead. But wait, the slight fluctuation of its chest, the slow blinking of its shiny black eyes. No, it was alive.

"Knife" (page 144)

I can do this by myself.

I held the blade, watched it slide across my flesh. The knife was just like Richard Selzer described: cold, gleaming, silent. Red drops of blood trailed the slightly serrated edge. I let out a long sigh.

Two Keys to Making This Kind of Opening Work

1. Make sure you give us context very soon after establishing the unusual image—maybe in the second paragraph. In a movie, if the viewers don't know what's happening, you'll lose them in about seven minutes—but college essay readers have a much shorter attention span, and if you keep yours in the dark for more than a paragraph or two, you're likely to lose them.

2. Don't use an image *solely* for its shock value. It can have shock value, but the image must be tied in some important way to one of the major themes or lessons of the story. In the "Dying Bird" essay, for example, the opening image functions in

several ways by (1) setting up the author's Want (to save the dying bird), which is the larger arc of the story, and (2) setting up the author's Need (to let the bird—and, by extension, her friend who died—go). For more on creating a Want vs. Need dynamic, see page 131.

IMPORTANT NOTE: Although both these openings begin with an unusual or striking image, they ALSO begin with a problem that must be solved.

Variation: Just Start Your Darn Essay

It's easy to obsess over finding the *perfect* essay opening and delay (read: stall, procrastinate) writing your essay until you've found that perfect beginning. Here's a secret: often, that opening is going to get rewritten because, once you write the middle of the essay, you discover the topic needs to change. Or you realize you need to start your essay at a later point in the story—right at the crucial moment of decision, for example.

So here's some advice for those looking for that perfect opening: just write your essay. Get started. You'll find an opening later.

Another secret: some of the best essays I've read didn't have mind-blowing openings. Some of the best essays start quietly. Examples:

"Grandma's Kimchi" (page 209)

Every Saturday morning, I'd awaken to the smell of crushed garlic and piquant pepper. I would stumble into the kitchen to find my grandma squatting over a large silver bowl, mixing fat lips of fresh cabbages with garlic, salt, and red pepper. That was how the delectable Korean dish, kimchi, was born every weekend at my home.

"Breaking Up with Mom" (page 192)

> I stare into my cappuccino to try to avoid looking at my teary eyed mom, who had just found a hole in her favorite bright pink floral print scarf.

"Barbie vs. Terrorism and the Patriarchy" (page 207)

> Much of my early knowledge of how the world works was formed through countless hours spent playing with Barbie dolls.

HOW DO I SHOW THE READER
I'M REALLY SMART?

IMPORTANT NOTE: The primary aim of your essay shouldn't be to prove your intelligence—it should be to demonstrate core values that are central to who you are. Also, if you're a smart person, trust that your intelligence will come through in your selection of topic, your articulation of your values, and your insights.

Having said this, here are some techniques that I've seen students use that really helped me see their intelligence. Just so I'm clear, though, this should not be where you primarily focus your attention. Don't just put lipstick on a pig. First, make sure you've got a really fine pig. Then consider the techniques presented here to be some different shades of lipstick to make that pig look fabulous.

Also, do not assume that just because you litter your paper with big words that you will sound really smart (see the "Use Big Words Selectively" section on page 199).

Method 1: Ask Great Questions

My favorite way that I've seen students demonstrate their intelligence in an essay isn't through smart statements—it's through smart questions. Take a look at these examples:

"Rock, Paper, Scissors" (page 169)

Rock beats scissors, scissors beats paper, and paper beats rock. Wait... paper beats rock? Since when has a sheet of loose leaf paper ever defeated a solid block of granite? Do we assume that the paper wraps around the rock, smothering the rock into submission? When exposed to paper, is rock somehow immobilized, unable to fulfill its primary function of smashing scissors? What constitutes defeat between two inanimate objects?

Such great questions. Two possible benefits of smart questions:

1. You can help the reader see something ordinary in a new and unusual way.
2. Your questions might inspire the reader's imagination, making him or her wonder how you'll answer those questions.

But there's another value to asking questions:

"Endodontics" (page 24)

As a kid I was always curious. I was unafraid to ask questions and didn't worry how dumb they would make me sound. In second grade I enrolled in a summer science program and built a solar-powered oven that baked real cookies. I remember obsessing over the smallest details: Should I paint the oven black to absorb more heat? What about its shape? A spherical shape would allow for more volume, but would it trap heat as well as conventional rectangular ovens? Even then I was obsessed with the details of design.

Notice how these questions demonstrate the core value of this paragraph: curiosity. And while these may not be mind-blowing questions, they sure are smart—especially for a second grader.

And here's one more great thing about questions—you don't have to actually answer them in your essay. Here's what I mean...

"With Debate" (page 22)

> In particular, I am interested in the North-South Korean tension. What irreconcilable differences have prompted a civilization to separate? Policy implications remain vague, and sovereignty theories have their limits—how do we determine what compromises are to be made? And on a personal level, why did my grandfather have to flee from his destroyed North Korean hometown—and why does it matter?

See? These questions don't get answered here. Why? They'd be impossible to answer in a thorough way in such a short personal statement—and that's totally fine. Just ask the questions and make sure, as this writer has done, that your questions are complex enough that they might engage your interest through college and beyond.

Fun fact: This writer didn't have these questions in her head when she started writing this essay. She had to do some research.

Tip: Research your topic to discover what other smart questions people in your intended field of study are asking or have already asked. Then use those questions to inspire your own.

Method 2: Use Geeky Language

If you know a subject really well, and can speak about it in ways that are shining, shimmering, and splendid, then go for it.

Just Enough Geeky Language

Through switch-side policy debate I not only discuss a multitude of competing ideas, but also argue from both sides of widely disputed issues. By equipping me with Protagoras' antilogic and Dissoi Logoi, switch-side policy debate has provided me with a forum to cultivate a diversity of intellectual perspectives that has informed my own intellectual growth.

Notice how the writer uses a bit of jargon to demonstrate that he knows some stuff about some stuff.

But don't use so much jargon that you alienate the reader. Here's what I mean:

Too Much Geeky Language

The first project that I was involved with investigated the extraintestinal manifestations of IBD. Patients who suffer from IBD often have diseases called extraintestinal manifestations that also affect multiple other organ systems and can be just as, if not more debilitating than the intestinal inflammation itself. My contribution involved examining data in Dr. Shih's clinical database, which led me to discover that the skin is one of the most commonly affected organ systems in patients who suffer from IBD. I contributed to Dr. Shih's review article to give an overview of the types of skin diseases typically seen with IBD and their respective pathogenesis, proposed mechanisms, and treatments, and my contributions were significant enough to earn recognition as a second author.

Using too much jargon can leave the reader wondering: *Who cares? What's the takeaway?*

> Tip: To avoid going overboard with jargon, insert a phrase after your geeky language that helps contextualize things for the reader.

"Endodontics" (Geeky Language + "So What")

I'm the math geek who marvels at the fundamental theorems of Calculus, or who sees beauty in $A = (s(s - a)(s - b)(s - c))^{(1 / 2)}$. Again, it's in the details: one bracket off or one digit missing and the whole equation collapses. **And details are more than details, they can mean the difference between negative and positive infinity, an impossible range of solutions.**

This is great because we get the geeky language, but we also get some insight into why this is a big deal for the writer—so we learn something more about the writer than just that he or she is smart.

Method 3: Show First, Then Tell

"Show, don't tell" is another phrase you've probably heard from your English teacher. It's an invitation to use images (i.e., create a pretty picture) to illustrate ideas, which is a good starting point. But I think a college admissions officer is interested in not only the pretty picture you paint, but also your reflections and insights on what the pretty picture means to you, the writer. Let me show you what I mean.

Here's an example of a nice "show," again from the "Endodontics" essay:

Many nights you'll find me in the garage replacing standard chrome trim with an elegant piano black finish or changing the threads on the stitching of the seats to add a personal touch...

Great start. But if the writer stops there, we're not sure what his perspective on these details is. That's why I advocate for a little "tell" after the "show."

Example of "show" followed by "tell":

> Many nights you'll find me in the garage replacing standard chrome trim with an elegant piano black finish or changing the threads on the stitching of the seats to add a personal touch, **as I believe a few small changes can transform a generic product into a personalized work of art.**

The "show" demonstrates you're a talented writer.

The "tell" demonstrates you're a critical thinker.

Be both.

Analogy of the Painter, the Art Critic, and the Curator

Consider that, in a college essay:

- the painter is in charge of creating the beautiful images
- the art critic is in charge of saying smart stuff about the images

So, when dreaming up beautiful images and examples for your essay, think of yourself as a painter.

But here's the thing: your responsibility is to also be the art critic, in charge of saying something smart about the images. Your goal is to illuminate something about the work that we might otherwise miss.

And what if you don't have anything smart to say about the image? That's the best part:

You are also the curator, in charge of deciding whether the image/example stays or goes. And you can elect to change out the painting at any time…preferably for an image/example about which you do have something smart/interesting/illuminating to say.

TIP: Put the "show" <u>before</u> the "tell," as opposed to the other way around.

Version A (Show before Tell)

Many nights you'll find me in the garage replacing standard chrome trim with an elegant piano black finish or changing the threads on the stitching of the seats to add a personal touch, **as I believe a few small changes can transform a generic product into a personalized work of art.**

Version B (Tell before Show)

I believe a few small changes can transform a generic product into a personalized work of art, which is why many nights you'll find me in the garage replacing standard chrome trim with an elegant piano black finish or changing the threads on the stitching of the seats to add a personal touch.

See how Version A is a little better?

Putting the images (show) before your interpretation of them (tell) accomplishes two things:

1. It creates an interesting puzzle in the reader's mind: What do these images mean? What will they add up to? This engages the reader's imagination.
2. Once you deliver your interpretation, the specificity of your articulation will be more surprising because it will be something the reader won't have thought of (and by the way, make sure it's something the reader won't have thought of).

And the way you can ensure this is by choosing images and examples that you can provide insight about—that's your job as curator. And what is insight? It's something you see that the reader doesn't.

Tip: Include "insight" moments three to five times in your essay. (Look at the "Endodontics" essay on page 24 and see if you can spot how many times he offers insights. Hint: Look at the ends of his paragraphs.)

HOW DO I BRAG WITHOUT SEEMING LIKE I'M BRAGGING?

Let's be honest. If there were ever a time to talk about how awesome you are, it's in your college application. But how do you do it in a way that doesn't sound like that's all you're doing? Here's my advice:

Connect your achievement or skill to an important value.

What do I mean? Weave your brag into a paragraph that is really (or primarily) about something else.

Examples:

"With Debate" (page 22)

More importantly, I now confront issues instead of avoiding them. It is exciting to discover solutions to problems that affect others, as I was able to do as part of the 1st Place team for the 2010 United Nations Global Debates Program on climate change and poverty. I take a natural interest in global issues, and plan to become a foreign affairs analyst or diplomat by studying international affairs with a focus on national identity.

Note that this paragraph is primarily about how the author has developed courage and is discovering solutions to problems that affect others, so her fancy UN Global Debates award isn't (only) a brag, it's evidence that she has developed, or is in the process of developing, this value.

"Endodontics" (page 24)

I also love sharing this appreciation with others and have taken it upon myself to personally eradicate mathonumophobiconfundosis, my Calculus teacher's term for "extreme fear of Math." A small group of other students and I have devoted our after-school time to tutoring our peers in everything from Pre-Algebra to AP Calculus B/C and I believe my fluency in Hebrew and Farsi has helped me connect with some of my school's Israeli and Iranian students. There's nothing better than seeing a student solve a difficult problem without me saying anything.

Same technique: this paragraph is primarily about helping others. But the author works in a brag (his ability to speak Hebrew and Farsi) by connecting it to this value—in other words, his fluency in multiple languages has helped him pursue this deeper (and altruistic) value.

Note on technique: See how in both these examples the important value is established in the first sentence of the paragraph? That's good. You don't have to do this, of course, but it can really help make the value clear, especially if you're about to slide in an "Oh, by the way, I'm a rock star" detail.

HOW DO I MAKE MY ESSAY, LIKE, DEEP?

Here are two ways to add depth and complexity to your essay:

Method 1: Feelings and Needs Exercise

This first exercise is adapted from an exercise inspired by Nonviolent Communication (NVC), which is a communication process that supposes that we all have the same needs, and when we can identify those needs and the feelings surrounding those needs, we become better equipped to communicate about our experiences. In NVC, this can lead to a higher likelihood of our getting our needs met. In college essay writing, it can lead to a higher likelihood of writing an awesome essay.

The purpose of this exercise is to take you deeper into your experiences and help you metabolize them by thinking about how your experiences led to feelings and needs that you worked to meet in creative ways. Sound abstract? Don't worry, we're about to get really specific. And I'll explain the steps of the exercise first, then offer a worksheet that you can fill out, if you like.

As before, if you don't feel you've experienced difficulties in life, simply replace "challenge" or "challenges" with the word "experience" or "experiences."

Take a blank sheet of paper, turn it sideways (horizontally), and write these words along the top:

1. Challenges	2. Effects	3. Feelings	4. Needs	5. What I Did	6. Other Values I Gained

If you've done an outline for "How to Write Essay Type A" on page 40, this may look similar, but this version is more comprehensive and it's the key to making your essay, like, deep.

HERE'S WHAT TO WRITE IN EACH COLUMN:

Column 1: Challenges
Write a challenge or a few challenges you've faced in your life, and then…

Column 2: Effects
Write the things that happened to you as a result of your challenge(s). In other words, the repercussions.

If you're unsure what I mean by "Challenges" and "Effects," and you skipped the "How to Write Essay Type A" section, go to page 40 for an explanation.

Note that most students list more than just two challenges, and I invite you to do the same. Take some time with this; it's really worth spending five to ten minutes per column.

Okay, here's where I invite you to be a little vulnerable.

Column 3: Feelings

Make a list of emotions that you felt as a result of the effects you've listed in column 2.

If it would help to see a list emotions—and it always helps me, since they're weirdly difficult to think of on the spot—take a look at the Feelings and Needs Exercise worksheet on page 127. And I'm so grateful that NVC expert LaShelle Lowe-Chardé (http://www .wiseheartpdx.org/) has allowed me to adapt her exercise for our purposes in this chapter.

> Tip: Don't move on until you've completed column 3.

In fact, here's a little white space to remind you to actually do this step and not read ahead.

Have you created your list of feelings?

Do you promise?

Okay, so far your brainstorm might look something like this:

1. Challenges	2. Effects	3. Feelings
Moved around a lot	No security or "home"	Anxious, lonely, stressed
Stuck in between cultures	Family shame, ridicule	Isolated, disconnected

Next step:

Column 4: Needs

Broadly speaking, Nonviolent Communication posits that when we feel negative emotions, it's due to an unmet need. So for each feeling you've listed, ask yourself, *What need wasn't being met?*

Examples

Let's say you moved around a lot (**Challenge**), which resulted in having no security or "home" (**Effect**), which led to your feeling anxious, lonely, and stressed (**Feelings**). Maybe what you lacked was consistency and stability (**Needs**), so you'd write those in column 4.

Or let's say that, growing up, you felt stuck between cultures (**Challenge**), which led to shame and ridicule (**Feelings**), causing you to feel isolated and disconnected (**Feelings**). It could be that your unmet needs were community and support.

So, right now, take a few minutes to brainstorm the unmet needs that may have been motivating each of the emotions listed in column 3.

To help you brainstorm, complete the Feelings and Needs Exercise on page 121.

Did you do it? Promise?

Okay, before moving on, let's go one level deeper.

Did you identify any emotions or needs that *surprised* you? Here's what I mean: sometimes we think we understand our past, but it's not until someone questions us that we realize that *there are multiple ways of making sense of our past*—some of which are unexpected.

Here's an example from my own life: if you'd asked me ten years ago what I thought of my parents' divorce, I'd have probably said, "Whatever, I didn't really feel any particular way about it."

But when I did this exercise I realized something...

When I, Ethan, experienced...my parents' divorce

I felt...disconnected and detached

Because I needed...intimacy, community, and connection.

And, I kid you not, I had this realization *while I was leading this exercise in front of a class*. I was like, "Whoa, didn't think about it that way." But it helped me better understand myself.

So here's my challenge: spend one more minute with this and ask yourself, "Are there any emotions or needs that might actually surprise me?" Maybe you skipped over something the first time, but once you went back and thought about it a little more you realized, "Oh wait... Yeah, I kinda *did* feel that" or "Maybe I *did* need that."

My challenge to you is this: **take a moment here**. Maybe close your eyes, take a deep breath, and feel into this. (I know, that's counseling talk, but go with me here.)

Take a few moments to meditate on this until you make a realization. It could be the key to your whole essay.

More white space because I really want you to do this.

Okay, next:

Column 5: What I Did

What did you do to meet your unmet need(s)? In my case, in order to meet my need for connection, community, and intimacy, I got involved in theater. As my parents were divorcing, I became much more involved with my theater friends—both in and out of school—and essentially formed a new family. I found my community. I didn't know at the time that this was connected to my parents' divorce, but when I look back, it makes a lot of sense.

And you may be thinking, *Well, I didn't actually do anything to try to meet that need; I just lived my life.* But think about things in a broader sense. For example, I initially thought I got more involved in theater just because I liked acting in and writing plays, but when I thought about theater for a bit (seriously, while doing this exercise), I realized that theater really did help me meet my unmet needs.

So here you can either (a) list some things you know you did to meet your needs, or (b) list some of your favorite activities and ask, "Could it be that [this activity] was helping me meet my deeper needs? If so, which one(s)?" Spend a few minutes with this.

Column 6: Other Values I Gained

In my case, by joining theater I not only met my need for intimacy/community, I also found new ways to express my creativity (performing, writing), I gained the confidence to apply to one of the top universities for theater in the country, and I even got to travel to New York City and perform on a Broadway stage. So, in a weird, roundabout way, my parents' divorce helped me cultivate my passion for theater and the arts. Thanks, Mom and Dad!

So make a list of skills/qualities/values you developed in column 6.

If you need ideas, take a look once more at the "What Did I Learn" part of the Feelings and Needs Exercise that follows.

FEELINGS AND NEEDS EXERCISE

When I experienced_____,
I felt_____,
because I needed_____.

FEELINGS

Delighted	Healthy	Peaceful	Hurt	Shocked
Joyful	Empowered	Tranquil	Pain	Disturbed
Happy	Alive	Serene	Agony	Stunned
Amused	Robust	Calm	Anguish	Alarmed
Adventurous			Heartbroken	Appalled
Blissful	**Relaxed**	**Confident**	Lonely	Concerned
Elated	Relieved	Secure		Horrified
	Rested	Safe	**Depressed**	
Thankful	Mellow	Hopeful	Disconnected	**Sad**
Appreciative	At ease		Detached	Grief
Moved	Light	**Scared**	Despondent	Despair
Touched		Apprehensive	Dejected	Gloomy
Tender	**Content**	Dread	Bored	Sullen
Expansive	Cheerful	Worried		Downhearted
Grateful	Glad	Panicky	**Tired**	Hopeless
	Comfortable	Frightened	Burned out	
Excited	Pleased	Vulnerable	Exhausted	**Torn**
Enthusiastic			Lethargic	Ambivalent
Overjoyed	**Friendly**	**Nervous**		Confused
Fervent	Affectionate	Jittery	**Angry**	Puzzled
Giddy	Loving	Anxious	Furious	
Eager	Passionate	Restless	Rage	**Jealous**
Ecstatic		Vulnerable	Irate	Envious
Thrilled	**Energetic**		Resentful	Bitter
	Exhilarated	**Tense**	Irritated	
Satisfied	Exuberant	Cranky		**Embarrassed**
Fulfilled	Vigorous	Stiff	**Frustrated**	Ashamed
Gratified		Stressed	Disappointed	Contrite
	Alert	Overwhelmed	Discouraged	Guilty
Interested	Focused	Agitated	Disheartened	
Curious	Awake		Impatient	
Absorbed	Clearheaded			

NEEDS

Intimacy
Empathy
Connection
Affection
Warmth
Love
Understanding
Acceptance
Caring
Bonding
Compassion
Communion
Divine union
Sexuality

Autonomy
Choice
Freedom
Spontaneity
Independence
Respect
Honor

Security
Predictability
Consistency
Stability
Trust
Reassurance

Partnership
Mutuality
Friendship
Companionship
Support
Collaboration
Belonging
Community
Consideration
Seen/Heard
Appreciation

Purpose
Competence
Contribution
Efficiency
Growth
Learning
Challenge
Discovery

Order
Structure
Clarity
Focus
Information

Celebration
Aliveness
Humor
Beauty
Play
Creativity
Joy
Mourning

Honesty
Integrity
Authenticity
Wholeness
Fairness

Peace
Groundedness
Hope
Healing
Harmony

Nurturing
Food/Water
Rest/Sleep
Safety
Shelter

WHAT DID I DO ABOUT IT?

To meet the need(s) just mentioned, I _____.

(What did you do? Example: I learned time management.)

If you're still in process (i.e., haven't done anything yet), what could you do to meet those needs?

As a result, I developed _____.

(What values did you develop? Choose a few from the list that follows.)

Again, if you haven't done anything yet, what values do you antic-
ipate developing?

WHAT DID I LEARN?

Community	Excellence	Meditation
Inspiration	Meaning	Practicality
Serenity	Power	Creativity
Physical challenge	Privacy	Excitement
Responsibility	Self-expression	Collaboration
Competition	Stability	Social change
Career	Diversity	Beauty
Practicality	Love	Passion
Working with others	Control	Integrity
Freedom	Surprise	Ecological awareness
Security	Nutrition	Quality relationships
Strength	Competence	Travel
Self-control	Risk	Logic
Hunger	Balance	Curiosity
Personal development	Self-discipline	Spirituality
Respect	Courage	Directness
Mindfulness	Family	Honesty
Culture	Empathy	Independence
Bravery	Working alone	Multiplicity
Communication	Fun	Supervising others
Change and variety	Humility	Cooperation
Compassion	Efficiency	Affection
Nature	Intensity	Wisdom
Intuition	Health and fitness	Knowledge
Trust	Meaningful work	Growth
Social justice	My country	Mystery
Intellect	Music	Order
Self-reliance	Truth	Innovation
Financial gain	Resourcefulness	Accountability
Laughter	Awareness	Democracy
Faith	Art	Religion
Involvement	Autonomy	Experience
Adventure	Wit	_____
Vulnerability	Patience	_____
Adaptability	Listening	_____
Restraint	Commitment	_____
Healthy boundaries	Leadership	_____
Friendship	Helping others	_____

What to Do Next: Start Making Some Connections

Once you've filled in all the columns, see if you can formulate a sentence or two that connects all the columns:

1. Challenges   2. Effects   3. Feelings   4. Needs   5. What I Did   6. Other Values I Gained

Example from my own life (key points in bold): After my **parents' divorce**, we spent less time together as a family, which led to me feeling somewhat **detached** and **disconnected**. I think deep down I needed **intimacy, connection,** and **belonging**. During this time, I got more involved with the **theater** program at my school, and not only found the **community** that I wanted, but also became more **independent** and **creative**. I even got the chance to **travel** to New York City.

If You Know Your Future Career...

Feel free to connect the "Other Values I Gained" to your career at the end of your essay—you might even create one more column right now, if you like, to brainstorm some connections. For more ideas on how to do this, see "How to Write Essay Type A" on page 40.

Once you've done this, chances are you should have a thread or two that will connect your story elements. As with the type A and type C approaches, I'd recommend using narrative structure to outline your essay.

If you'd like to see example essays that are "deep"—and by "deep," I mean essays in which the author discusses a deeper need—check out the "Porcelain God," "Easter," "What I Found on the Farm," "Knife," and "Breaking Up with Mom" essays. There are other essays in the book that do this, but I think these are the clearest examples.

The "Burying Grandma" essay discussed in the next section addresses a deeper need, but the author takes a slightly different approach to structuring the essay.

Method 2: Setting Up a Want vs. Need Dynamic

Here's a screenwriting secret: in most popular films you've seen, there are two stories unfolding.

1. The Outside Story: These are the external circumstances of the story, typically the main plot.
2. The Inside Story: The main character's inner journey, typically some sort of emotional shift marked by a realization that the way he or she has been doing things has been wrong (or at least not ideal).

Examples:

Star Wars

- Outside Story: Luke wants to keep the universe from being taken over by the Dark Side.
- Inside Story: Luke needs to learn to believe in himself in order to use The Force.

Finding Nemo

- Outside Story: Nemo's dad, Marlin, wants to find Nemo.
- Inside Story: Marlin needs to overcome his overprotective nature and ultimately let Nemo go.

Toy Story

- Outside Story: Woody wants to get rid of Buzz Lightyear so that Woody can go back to being Andy's favorite toy.
- Inside Story: Instead of getting Buzz out, Woody needs to get over his jealousy and, essentially, let Buzz in.

Notice the way I've phrased those:

- Outside Story = main character's **want**
- Inside Story = main character's **need**

Here's another way of thinking about this:

- What the movie is about on the surface = **Outside Story/want**
- What the film is *really* about = **Inside Story/need**

And that's what gives these films depth, *particularly if the want and need are, at some point in the story, in direct opposition.* Look at *Toy Story* and *Finding Nemo*, for example. In both cases, the main character spends the first part of the movie pursuing the thing he thinks is going to make him happy (getting rid of Buzz Lightyear, finding Nemo). But we, the wise audience members, know that there's a deeper lesson the character needs to learn (to accept Buzz Lightyear, to let Nemo go).

What does this have to do with your essay?

Ask yourself this question: Was there ever a time in your life when you were pursuing one thing (a want), but once you thought about it, you realized there was something deeper that you were really searching for (a need)?

It's kind of a huge question. In fact, you probably didn't just read that and think, "Oh yeah, totally." It takes some thought, and sometimes even a little creative reframing. But if you can do this, it can add real dimension to your essay.

Several of the sample essays in this book employ this want/need dynamic, and I don't think all the authors knew they were doing it. Take a look:

"With Debate" (Type A)

> **Want**: to get over her shyness, which she does by joining debate and coming out of her shell

> **Need**: to accept her shyness—rather than try to get over it—and ultimately accept that she isn't two separate parts, but one whole being...just as "the Korean civilization is also one," as she says in the last paragraph

"I Shot My Brother" (Type C)

> **Want**: to get rid of his brother (on a subconscious level, it could be argued, he wants to "kill" him)

> **Need**: to get over his jealousy and reconcile with his brother

"Dying Bird" (Type C)

> **External Want**: to save the bird

> **External Need**: to let the bird go

But the "Dying Bird" essay is particularly satisfying because it actually has a...

> **Deeper Want**: to save her friend

> **Deeper Need**: to let her friend go

That's next level stuff.

"Why Did the Chicken Cross the Road?"

Even this essay on page 162 has a version of the want/need dynamic at work.

Chicken's **want**: to get to the other side of the road

Chicken's **need**: to get back *from* the other side of the road

That's what makes that story so satisfying—it provides an ending that's surprising, but inevitable (see page 150 for more on this).

So How Do You Do This in Your Essay?

Notice that in each of the essays I just mentioned, there's a moment when the author shifts from pursuing his or her want to pursuing his or her need. Ask yourself: Could I work such a moment into my story?

The essay below provides a clear example. Try to identify the want, the need, and the moment when the shift happens.

"BURYING GRANDMA"

They covered the precious mahogany coffin with a brown amalgam of rocks, decomposed organisms, and weeds. It was my turn to take the shovel, but I felt too ashamed to dutifully send her off when I had not properly said goodbye. I refused to throw dirt on her. I refused to let go of my grandmother, to accept a death I had not seen coming, to believe that an illness could not only interrupt, but steal a beloved life.

When my parents finally revealed to me that my grandmother had been battling liver cancer, I was twelve and I was angry—mostly with myself. They had wanted to protect me—only six years old at the time—from the complex and morose concept of death. However, when the end inevitably arrived, I wasn't trying to comprehend what dying was; I was trying to understand how

I had been able to abandon my sick grandmother in favor of playing with friends and watching TV. Hurt that my parents had deceived me and resentful of my own oblivion, I committed myself to preventing such blindness from resurfacing.

I became desperately devoted to my education because I saw knowledge as the key to freeing myself from the chains of ignorance. While learning about cancer in school I promised myself that I would memorize every fact and absorb every detail in textbooks and online medical journals. And as I began to consider my future, I realized that what I learned in school would allow me to silence that which had silenced my grandmother. However, I was focused not with learning itself, but with good grades and high test scores. I started to believe that academic perfection would be the only way to redeem myself in her eyes—to make up for what I had not done as a granddaughter.

However, a simple walk on a hiking trail behind my house made me open my own eyes to the truth. Over the years, everything—even honoring my grandmother—had become second to school and grades. As my shoes humbly tapped against the Earth, the towering trees blackened by the forest fire a few years ago, the faintly colorful pebbles embedded in the sidewalk, and the wispy white clouds hanging in the sky reminded me of my small though nonetheless significant part in a larger whole that is humankind and this Earth. Before I could resolve my guilt, I had to broaden my perspective of the world as well as my responsibilities to my fellow humans.

Volunteering at a cancer treatment center has helped me discover my path. When I see patients trapped in not only the hospital but also a moment in time by their diseases, I talk to them. For six hours a day, three times a week, Ivana is surrounded by IV stands, empty walls, and busy nurses that quietly yet constantly remind her of her breast cancer. Her face is pale and tired, yet kind—not unlike my grandmother's. I need only to smile and say hello to see her brighten up as life returns to her face. Upon our first meeting, she opened up about her two sons, her hometown, and her knitting group—no mention of her disease. Without even standing up, the three of us—Ivana, me, and my grandmother—had taken a walk together.

Cancer, as powerful and invincible as it may seem, is a mere fraction of a person's life. It's easy to forget when one's mind and body are so weak and vulnerable. I want to be there as an oncologist to remind them to take a walk once in awhile, to remember that there's so much more to life than a disease. While I physically treat their cancer, I want to lend patients emotional support and mental strength to escape the interruption and continue living. Through my work, I can accept the shovel without burying my grandmother's memory.

So what was the author's want? What about her need?

There's no perfect answer here, but here's my version: the author's **want** was to deal with her guilt around her grandma's death by burying herself in her studies. Her **need** was to heal from her grandma's death by broadening "[her] perspective of the world," as she puts it, "as well as [her] responsibilities to [her] fellow humans," something she ends up doing through her volunteer work at the hospital.

Here are two tips for applying this technique:

1. Once you've shifted from the want to the need, demonstrate what you did about it. Think, for example, how that essay would be different if she'd ended it with this sentence: "Before I could resolve my guilt, I had to broaden my perspective of the world as well as my responsibilities to my fellow humans." We wouldn't get a chance to see that she actually externalized the lesson—that she actually did something about it.

2. For the first part of the essay, try solving your problem in a "bad" way (by pursuing the want), then include a turning

point/realization and begin to work on your problem in a "good" way (pursuing the need).

Finally, if you're writing a type B or D essay, you may be wondering if these two methods for adding depth apply mostly to type A and C (challenges) essays. Yes, they do, since both exercises rely on challenges. If you'd like to add depth and complexity to a type B essay, either turn to page 196 to learn how to make sure your insights are actually insightful, or turn to page 68 to learn how to combine narrative and montage structures by including a challenge in a montage essay.

HOW DO I END MY ESSAY?

The best endings have two things in common. And I won't make you guess what they are; I'll just tell you.

The best endings are surprising, but inevitable.

Take a look at two examples from essays in this book.

At the end of the "Endodontics" essay, the author reveals that he wants to study dentistry (specifically, endodontics). This is somewhat surprising, as we might have pegged him for an engineering guy. But when we look back at his essay, we see that the values he has been describing in the essay will actually make him a great dentist. So even though "endodontist" initially catches us off-guard, once we think about it (and once he makes that "machines" connection near the end), the ending feels, well, kind of inevitable.

The "Easter" essay begins with the author trapped (physically and psychologically) at home with her mother. At the end of the essay, the author notes that she will celebrate Easter again, but next time will be different—rather than being trapped indoors, she and her mother will celebrate outdoors their rebirth and renewal. In this case, what's surprising is that she brought up Easter again in the essay. But of course she did, since it's the perfect metaphor for the rebirth that she and her mother have experienced in the story. So, in a way, the ending feels inevitable.

Think about your favorite movie or play: you probably knew how it was going to end, but something about it still surprised you. Or, alternately, perhaps you had no idea how it was going to end. But once it was over, you thought, "Yeah, that makes sense."

Examples:

- You know by the end of every romantic comedy that the two main characters will end up together (it's inevitable); you're just waiting to find out *how* (and that's the surprising part).
- In every epic action film, you know that OF COURSE they'll save the planet before it's destroyed (that's inevitable), but you're still watching the film because you want to see *how* (that's the surprise).

Here's something to keep in mind: if your ending is too "inevitable," it means that we saw it coming a mile away, and it will feel boring, like the punch line to a bad joke. But, on the other hand, if the ending is too "surprising," then it probably means we didn't see it coming at all, and it might feel random. The key is the sweet spot in the middle:

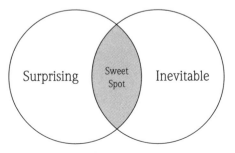

Are all great endings both surprising and inevitable?

No. The ending of the "Porcelain God" essay, for example, feels, at least to me, more inevitable than surprising. (I mean, come on, "my regular visits to my allergy specialist inspired me to become an allergy specialist." *Super* inevitable.) Also, as you read the "With Debate" essay, some part of you knew the author would inevitably overcome her shyness. But in both cases, there were elements at the end that were surprising. The "Porcelain God" author, for example, attended the program at Stanford (that's somewhat unexpected), while the "With Debate" author lays out a beautiful metaphor describing how the North–South Korean dividing line actually represents the introverted and extroverted parts of herself. So, while part of their stories may have been inevitable, what they say at the end answers "so what?" in a surprising way.

Keep that in mind, by the way: if this "surprising, but inevitable" technique seems too complex, just answer "so what" at the end of your essay, ideally in an unexpected way.

HOW TO WRITE A GREAT LAST LINE FOR YOUR ESSAY

Look at the final lines of some of the essays mentioned earlier. What do they all have in common?

→ "Endodontics" essay: *The question is: Will the toothbrushes I hand out be mineral white or diamond white?*

→ "Bowling" essay: *I know that one day I will not take my family to a bowling alley to clean it but to enjoy it. And who knows, maybe one day I will learn to bowl.*

→ "Easter" essay: *My Easter will drastically differ from past years. Rather than being locked at home, my mother and I will celebrate outdoors our rebirth and renewal.*

Cudgel thy brains no more about it, I'll tell you:

All these endings return to some earlier moment in the essay, but from a different perspective.

> T. S. Eliot put it best in the *Four Quartets:* "In my beginning is my end"
> and "In my end is my beginning."
> That's the goal.

You may still be wondering: How do I implement the "surprising, but inevitable" technique? Can I see an example in a full essay?

Yes, indeed. In fact, I'll give you three example essays that use this technique: "I Shot My Brother," "Dying Bird," and "Five Families." I analyze the first two in the "Four Qualities of an Amazing Essay" section that begins on page 178, and I analyze the third in the "Advanced Technique 4" section that begins on page 150.

But in order to understand the "surprising, but inevitable" concept fully, I recommend learning more about setup and payoff, which is the foundation of this approach and something I explain in the next chapter, "Advanced Techniques." Just one quick note before we get there on what to do if you're feeling like you're behind in the process.

WHAT DO I DO IF I FEEL LIKE I'M FALLING BEHIND?

You might be whizzing right along at this point and you're hard at work on your third or eighth draft. Good for you. But maybe you're not quite there yet—maybe you're still struggling to nail down your structure or even decide on your topic.

Listen, it's totally fine. You aren't falling behind. Writing is a strange and unpredictable process. The best thing you can do is to keep at it—keep reading, keep writing, and, above all, keep trying new things. What sorts of new things?

Here are a few ideas:

If you're still struggling to find your topic...

What's wrong with you? I'm kidding. Some options:

1. Try writing Morning Pages, as Julia Cameron suggests in *The Artist's Way,* which are three pages of longhand, stream-of-consciousness writing done first thing in the morning..
2. Have you tried brainstorming with a partner yet? If not, try it. Maybe you tried brainstorming with someone and it didn't work? Try someone else!
3. Just pick something and start writing. That simple? Yep. It's better than doing nothing.

You've Got Your Topic, but Aren't Sure That the Structure Is Right or That the Essay Flows

- First, go back to page 102 and review "How to Revise Your Essay in Five Steps."
- Repeat those steps until, when you read your essay aloud, you can hear the ideas flow together in a clear way.
- Get feedback from someone else. Does that person agree? Super. You're on your way.
- Maybe you asked someone else but didn't get useful feedback? Try another person. Keep going until you get the help you need.

Just Need Some Inspiration?

I have a whole website dedicated to college essay inspiration that I update weekly: http://collegeessayguy.tumblr.com/.

CHAPTER SEVEN

Advanced Techniques

MANY OF THE TOOLS DISCUSSED in this chapter come from screenwriting. Why? Because I have spent a whole lot of time studying screenwriting structure and have learned that screenwriting structure works *beautifully* for college essay structure. Oh, and because you've probably watched movies, and because the visual images you'll use in your essay will mean your essay is basically a short film.

Here are five techniques I call "advanced," not because they are necessarily difficult to understand, but because they can be a bit more difficult to do well. But if you can pull these off, the payoff can be big. Speaking of payoff…

ADVANCED TECHNIQUE 1: SETUP AND PAYOFF

Degree of difficulty: 5.2

Setup and payoff is a narrative technique that involves "setting up" a detail or a statement that initially seems irrelevant, and then later making the relevance very clear—in other words, "paying it off."

As Chekhov said:

If you say in the first chapter that there is a rifle hanging on the wall, in the second or third chapter it absolutely must go off.

It can also be useful to cut extraneous setups that promise or imply certain payoffs that never arrive. Here's the rest of that Chekhov quotation:

If [the gun is] not going to be fired, it shouldn't be hanging there.

Three Simple "Setup" Examples from Film

1. At the beginning of *The Wizard of Oz*, Dorothy sings "Somewhere Over the Rainbow." Guess where she goes?
2. At the opening of *Citizen Kane*, a dying man's last word is "Rosebud." Guess what "Rosebud" is? (Actually, I won't ruin it for you.)
3. A troll in *Frozen* explains that only an "act of true love" will prevent Anna's heart from freezing forever. And, well, you get it…

Who This Technique Is For

This technique is for:

a. students who have been through a particularly big change in their lives and are having difficulty finding a larger structure, or
b. any student looking to make his or her essay more interesting.

In short, this technique can be used to structure an entire essay (as the "Knife" essay that follows does) or small moments throughout the essay (as the "Knife" essay also does).

And here's an important qualifier: what the sample essay "Knife" attempts is extremely difficult, given the sensitivity of the topic, and I did not, for the record, advise the student to write about this. She wrote about it without consulting me, sent it to me, and when I read it, I thought, *This is incredibly risky, but the story is told so well that I feel she has truly moved through this and learned from it.* How risky was it? A colleague of mine and former admissions officer at Mills College noted that, after reading this essay, she would have had to flag it for the college's psychological services office, and there's no telling how many hands this essay would have had to pass through at Stanford, where the student was ultimately accepted.

Having said all this, her technique here is wonderful, and we can learn a lot from it. Read the essay first without my notes.

"KNIFE"

I can do this by myself.

I held the blade, watched it slide across my flesh. The knife was just like Richard Selzer described: cold, gleaming, silent. Red drops of blood trailed the slightly serrated edge. I let out a long sigh.

I was at my most desperate. My friend had died in September of my junior year. Five AP classes, weekly volunteering, and a tutoring job had provided added stress. I needed reprieve. And I found it in the knife.

Two months later, my French teacher, Madame Deleuze, discovered my secret. That day in AP French while everyone else drilled vocabulary, she called me out to have a talk.

Bubbly and smiling, I chatted about the test we were about to take.

"I know what you're doing, Sara. I know you cut yourself."

My breath caught in my throat. My hands grew cold. My pulse sped up. I looked down at my shoes, then at the green planter next to me. This can't be happening. I dug my nails into my hands to stop them from shaking. I began to cry.

Shame. I had wanted to be the perfect student, an effort-less model of fortitude. School, volunteering, work. I can do it. I will do it. Bring it on. I had wanted to be that girl, the teacher's pet, the lone wolf, the ambitious go-getter with big dreams and even bigger expectations. What I had not wanted to be was a victim.

But as Madame Deleuze held me, her voice cracking, she spoke words of compassion.

"You're beautiful. You're valuable. You're amazing and so, so precious. Don't ever let yourself think otherwise."

Enclosed in her arms, I realized that I had been a victim—a victim of my own relentless standards.

Since that day, my every flaw, my every hurt has been laid bare. My mother cried for hours when she first found out. My father said nothing. In fact, he remained silent for a week. My brother and my teachers were shocked. I seemed a stranger to them.

Yet in their despair, they chose to love me.

My mother drove me to therapy every week with tears staining her makeup. My father, though quiet, left me breakfast every morning when I woke up. My brother, a freshman at CalArts, sent me text messages and braved LA traffic every weekend to see me. Mrs. Risher gave me tight hugs. Mrs. Natanzi, my counselor, sat me down, concern marking her face.

Their compassion allowed me to replace ambition for passion. I quit Key Club, SADD, French Club. Passion grew for the written word, journalism, speech and debate. It led me away from the pharmacy to forensics, pathology, pediatrics.

Failure seemed less a tragedy, more an opportunity. To ask for help was not weakness. To endure alone was not strength.

I can't do this by myself. I don't need to.

Analysis of "Knife"

I can do this by myself.

Setup 1: This sets up the final line of the essay.

I held the blade, watched it slide across my flesh. The knife was just like Richard Selzer described: cold, gleaming, silent. Red drops of blood trailed the slightly serrated edge. I let out a long sigh.

Setup 2: This builds suspense, raises the stakes, and launches the question of the essay: How will she overcome this?

I was at my most desperate. My friend had died in September of my junior year. Five AP classes, weekly volunteering, and a tutoring job had provided added stress. I needed reprieve. And I found it in the knife.

Setup 3: *Uh-oh*, we think. *What's going to happen outside the room?* (Mini setup, which helps build suspense.)

Two months later, my French teacher, Madame Deleuze, discovered my secret. That day in AP French while everyone else drilled vocabulary, she called me out to have a talk. Bubbly and smiling, I chatted about the test we were about to take.

Setup 4: Establish that the narrator doesn't see this coming. (Dramatic irony.)

"I know what you're doing, Sara. I know you cut yourself." My breath caught in my throat. My hands grew cold. My pulse sped up. I looked down at my shoes, then at the green planter next to me. This can't be happening. I dug my nails into my hands to stop them from shaking. I began to cry.

Payoff for setups 3 and 4.

Great verisimilitude (see page 147).

Shame. I had wanted to be the perfect student, an effortless model of fortitude. School, volunteering, work. I can do it. I will do it. Bring it on. I had wanted to be that girl, the teacher's pet, the lone wolf, the ambitious go-getter with big dreams and even bigger expectations. What I had not wanted to be was a victim.

Setup 5: This echoes and amplifies setup 1. She goes from "can" to "will" and then "Bring it on."

(Unexpected) payoff for setups 3 and 4: We didn't expect the teacher to say this.

But as Madame Deleuze held me, her voice cracking, she spoke words of compassion.

"You're beautiful. You're valuable. You're amazing and so, so precious. Don't ever let yourself think otherwise."

Enclosed in her arms, I realized that I had been a victim—a victim of my own relentless standards.

First payoff for setup 1.

Since that day, my every flaw, my every hurt has been laid

bare. My mother cried for hours when she first found out. My father said nothing. In fact, he remained silent for a week. My brother and my teachers were shocked. I seemed a stranger to them.

This pays off setup 2 in that it shows the consequences of her actions. It's also setup 6.

Yet in their despair, they chose to love me.

My mother drove me to therapy every week with tears staining her makeup. My father, though quiet, left me breakfast every morning when I woke up. My brother, a freshman at CalArts, sent me text messages and braved LA traffic every weekend to see me. Mrs. Risher gave me tight hugs. Mrs. Natanzi, my counselor, sat me down, concern marking her face.

Major turning point in the essay.

Pays off setup 6.

Their compassion allowed me to replace ambition for passion. I quit Key Club, SADD, French Club. Passion grew for the written word, journalism, speech and debate. It led me away from the pharmacy to forensics, pathology, pediatrics.

Pays off setup 5.

Failure seemed less a tragedy, more an opportunity. To ask for help was not weakness. To endure alone was not strength.

I can't do this by myself. I don't need to.

Final and most satisfying payoff, as it pays off setup 1 (at the start) and its echo in setup 5 (in the middle), giving the essay a feeling of roundedness and a through line.

ADVANCED TECHNIQUE 2: VERISIMILITUDE

Degree of difficulty: 4.4

The word "verisimilitude" comes from Latin: *veri similis* means "like the truth." This technique involves the use of specific details to give the story the ring of truth. In the previous essay, a detail such as "slightly serrated edge [of the knife]" gives the sense that this was an actual knife and, by extension, that this story really happened. Verisimilitude can help bring a story to life in a way that makes us believe, and often feel, the story more.

Here's another example from the "Raising Anthony" essay on page 26:

> On one particularly hopeful afternoon I even tried to introduce him
> to books that I had read—but I learned I can't win every battle.

Why this moment feels so true to life: at this point in the story, everything is working well—the author is soaking in parenting videos, having her little brother formulate his own penalties, and following up on his homework—but this moment brings us back to earth. It's useful because it saves the essay from having an ending that sounds like a Hallmark card, in which everything works out perfectly.

And here's one more example, from the "Knife" essay you just read:

> My breath caught in my throat. My hands grew cold. My pulse
> sped up. I looked down at my shoes, then at the green planter
> next to me.

Why did the author choose a "green" planter—why not blue or red? Does green symbolize something—nature, perhaps, or safety, or even envy? No! She notes that it was a green planter because that was *the actual color of the actual planter.*

Here's one of my favorite quotations from Gustave Flaubert:

> If I say the stones are blue it is because blue is the precise word,
> believe me.

Read that again. It's a good one.

There are other wonderful moments of verisimilitude in the essays in this book, particularly in the "Grandma's Kimchi" (page 209) and "Breaking Up with Mom" (page 192) essays.

ADVANCED TECHNIQUE 3: TURN SOMETHING DARK INTO SOMETHING BEAUTIFUL

Degree of difficulty: 9.1

One more strategy the author of the "Knife" essay uses to address the difficult, not-often-talked-about topic of cutting is giving us insight into why she did it. How does she do so? Look again at the second paragraph. She makes it sound almost...well, beautiful. And, if you possess all parts of humanity inside you—if, in other words, there is a part of you deep down that has ever seen something that other people might think was "gross" and you've found yourself thinking "that's actually kind of interesting"—*you kind of get it.* I'm not suggesting that you would cut yourself, but you see her perspective. So that's one possibility:

Turn something dark into something beautiful.

But there's a larger lesson here. For students who are struggling to find a way to talk about a challenge that either they are ashamed of or that is stigmatized in our culture, here is my invitation:

Get creative.

You don't have to give a straightforward account of your challenges, and you certainly don't have to describe every gory detail. Choose your details. Find what's interesting or compelling, and select the pieces that connect to the values we can all relate to. In the "Knife" essay, for example, I believe the story isn't primarily about cutting; I believe it's about someone who pushed herself too hard (I've done that), who got some support, and who is beginning to learn to accept help from others, which is something I (and perhaps you) can really relate to. In short:

Find what's universal about your experience.

That's something this author does very well in her essay, and it's a big part of why I think the essay works.

Although this student did end up at Stanford, I caution anyone against drawing too direct a conclusion from this, such as, "If I write about something really deep and dark, then I'll get into Stanford" or "This essay is why she got into Stanford." Why? Because her 2320 SAT score and near-perfect grades had a lot to do with her acceptance. But I offer this tidbit to note that it is possible to write about a topic like this and still be accepted to a great school. But, as I noted, the degree of difficulty is much higher.

ADVANCED TECHNIQUE 4: BLOW THE READER'S MIND BY USING *THE SIXTH SENSE* ENDING (A.K.A. CREATE AN ENDING THAT'S SURPRISING, BUT INEVITABLE)

Degree of difficulty: 7.5

Okay, we're about to take this setup and payoff thing to the next level.

Have you seen *The Sixth Sense*? Because I'm about to ruin it for you.

Haley Joel Osment's character sees dead people.

I'm kidding. Well, I'm not kidding, but you knew that. Actually, I'm about to give a plot summary, so if you haven't seen the film, consider watching it. But if you won't watch it, or don't care if I spoil the ending, read on.

Short Plot Summary of *The Sixth Sense*

The life of psychologist Dr. Crowe, played by Bruce Willis, changes forever when a disgruntled former patient walks into his house one night and puts a bullet in his gut (**Inciting Incident**). Soon after recovery, Crowe begins seeing a new patient named Cole, played by Haley Joel Osment, who swears he sees dead people (**Raise the Stakes**). Dr. Crowe, who seems to have trouble opening his basement office (**Setup**), tries to diagnose Cole, only to realize that he is telling the truth—he does actually see dead people (**Raise the Stakes Even More**). Dr. Crowe agrees to help Cole resolve these ghosts' problems so they can finally be at peace (**Turning Point**).

At the end of the film, Dr. Crowe goes home to his wife, whom he had estranged by working too hard. She drifts off to sleep while watching their wedding video. Then his wedding ring slips out of her fingers. Dr. Crowe, not remembering ever taking it off, realizes that he has actually been dead the whole time (**Payoff and another Turning Point**) and TA DA! Multiple story elements suddenly make more sense given this bit of information—even moments that you didn't even think about before. (So *that's* why Dr. Crowe talks to Cole only when they're alone! *That's* why he couldn't open the basement office door!)

What Can We Learn from This Technique?

The key moment—the final reveal at the end—works like any great "Whodunit" mystery in that it "pays off" all these little clues that have been buried or hidden along the way. In a well-made film, we don't make sense of these hints until the final reveal, which, as screenwriting teacher Robert McKee points out, is like a giant explosion that detonates all these little explosions in our minds and sends us mentally hurtling back through the film to connect all the hints that we were only partially aware of along the way.

And, if done really well:

It's *surprising* as in, "I totally didn't see that coming."

But it's *inevitable*, as in, "Now that I think about it, of *course* that's how it had to end."

> Fun fact: Almost every single example essay in this book has a conclusion that is somehow both surprising and inevitable.

If you can achieve both, you've got a winner. How can you do this? Two tips:

1. Set up your hints so that they're clear enough to be remembered at the payoff moment, but also buried enough so that we don't expect the payoff.

How do you "bury" them? Here's an idea:

2. Give us something else to focus on, or something that's interesting enough to capture our attention so we're not aware that you're burying a hint. It's kind of like a magic trick; it's a misdirect.

Want a clear example with some analysis?

I'll give you a whole essay. Read the "Five Families" essay that follows and see if you can spot the buried hints along the way. There's something toward the end that connects all the separate parts of the story.

I'll let you read it first without analysis so you can just enjoy it. Then we'll dissect it together.

"FIVE FAMILIES"

When I was 16, I lived with the Watkins family in Wichita, Kansas. Mrs. Watkins was the coordinator of the foreign exchange student program I was enrolled in. She had a nine year old son named Cody. I would babysit Cody every day after school for at least two to three hours. We would play Scrabble or he would read to me from *Charlotte's Web* or *The Ugly Duckling*. He would talk a lot about his friends and school life, and I would listen to him and ask him the meanings of certain words. He was my first friend in the New World.

My second family was the Martinez family, who were friends of the Watkins's. The host dad Michael was a high school English teacher and the host mom Jennifer (who had me call her "Jen") taught elementary school. She had recently delivered a baby, so she was still in the hospital when I moved into their house. The Martinez family did almost everything together. We made pizza together, watched *Shrek* on their cozy couch together, and went fishing on Sunday together. On rainy days, Michael, Jen and I would sit on the porch and listen to the rain, talking about our dreams and thoughts. Within two months I was calling them mom and dad.

After I finished the exchange student program, I had the option of returning to Korea but I decided to stay in America. I wanted to see new places and meet different people. Since I wasn't an exchange student anymore, I had the freedom— and burden—of finding a new school and host family on my own. After a few days of thorough investigation, I found the Struiksma family in California. They were a unique group.

The host mom Shellie was a single mom who had two of her own sons and two Russian daughters that she had adopted. The kids always had something warm to eat, and were always on their best behavior at home and in school. It would be fair to say that this was all due to Shellie's upbringing. My room was on the first floor, right in front of Shellie's hair salon, a small business that she ran out of her home. In the living room were six or seven huge amplifiers and a gigantic chandelier hung from the high ceiling. The kitchen had a bar. At first, the non-stop visits from strangers made me nervous, but soon I got used to them. I remember one night, a couple barged into my room while I was sleeping. It was awkward.

After a few months I realized we weren't the best fit. In the nicest way possible, I told them I had to leave. They understood.

The Ortiz family was my fourth family. Kimberly, the host mom, treated me the same way she treated her own son. She made me do chores: I fixed dinner, fed their two dogs Sassy and Lady, and once a week I cleaned the bathroom. I also had to follow some rules: No food in my room, no using the family computer, no lights on after midnight, and no ride unless it was an emergency. The first couple of months were really hard to get used to, but eventually I adjusted.

I lived with the Ortiz family for seven months like a monk in the deep forest. However, the host dad Greg's asthma got worse after winter, so he wanted to move to the countryside. It was unexpected and I only had a week to find a new host family. I asked my friend Danielle if I could live with her until I found a new home. That's how I met the Dirksen family, my fifth family.

The Dirksen family had three kids. They were all different. Danielle liked bitter black coffee, Christian liked energy drinks, and Becca liked sweet lemon tea. Dawn, the host mom didn't like winter, and Mark, the host dad, didn't like summer. After dinner, we would all play Wii Sports together. I was the king of bowling, and Dawn was the queen of tennis. I don't remember a single time that they argued about the games. Afterward, we would gather in the living room and Danielle would play the piano while the rest of us sang hymns.

Of course, those 28 months were too short to fully understand all five families, but I learned from and was shaped by each of them. By teaching me English, nine year-old Cody taught me the importance of being able to learn from anyone;

the Martinez family showed me the value of spending time together as a family; the Struiksma family taught me to reserve judgment about divorced women and adopted children; Mrs. Ortiz taught me the value of discipline and the Dirksen family taught me the importance of appreciating one another's different qualities.

Getting along with other people is necessary for anyone and living with five families has made me more sensitive to others' needs: I have learned how to recognize when someone needs to talk, when I should give advice and when to simply listen, and when someone needs to be left alone; in the process, I have become much more adaptable. I'm ready to change, learn, and be shaped by my future families.

Analysis of "Five Families"

When I was 16, I lived with the Watkins family in Wichita, Kansas. Mrs. Watkins was the coordinator of the foreign exchange student program I was enrolled in. She had a nine year old son named Cody. I would babysit Cody every day after school for at least two to three hours. We would play Scrabble or he would read to me from *Charlotte's Web* or *The Ugly Duckling*. He would talk a lot about his friends and school life, and I would listen to him and ask him the meanings of certain words. He was my first friend in the New World.

Is this just a sweet image? Or Top Secret Buried Hint 1? Both.

My second family was the Martinez family, who were friends of the Watkins's. The host dad Michael was a high school English teacher and the host mom Jennifer (who had me call her "Jen") taught elementary school. She had recently delivered a baby, so she was still in the hospital when I moved into their house. The Martinez family did almost everything together. We made pizza together, watched *Shrek* on their cozy

Hint 2.

couch together, and went fishing on Sunday together. On rainy days, Michael, Jen and I would sit on the porch and listen to the rain, talking about our dreams and thoughts. Within two months I was calling them mom and dad.

After I finished the exchange student program, I had the option of returning to Korea but I decided to stay in America. I wanted to see new places and meet different people. Since I wasn't an exchange student anymore, I had the freedom— and burden—of finding a new school and host family on my own. After a few days of thorough investigation, I found the Struiksma family in California. They were a unique group.

The host mom Shellie was a single mom who had two of her own sons and two Russian daughters that she had adopted. The kids always had something warm to eat, and were always on their best behavior at home and in school. It would be fair to say that this was all due to Shellie's upbringing. My room was on the first floor, right in front of Shellie's hair salon, a small business that she ran out of her home. In the living room were six or seven huge amplifiers and a gigantic chandelier hung from the high ceiling. The kitchen had a bar. At first, the non-stop visits from strangers made me nervous, but soon I got used to them. I remember one night, a couple barged into my room while I was sleeping. It was awkward.

After a few months I realized we weren't the best fit. In the nicest way possible, I told them I had to leave. They understood.

The Ortiz family was my fourth family. Kimberly, the host mom, treated me the same way she treated her own son. She made me do chores: I fixed dinner, fed their two dogs Sassy and Lady, and once a week I cleaned the bathroom. I also had to follow some rules: No food in my room, no using the family computer, no lights on after midnight, and no ride unless it was an emergency. The first couple of months were really hard to get used to, but eventually I adjusted.

Hint 3.

Hint 4.

I lived with the Ortiz family for seven months like a monk in the deep forest. However, the host dad Greg's asthma got worse after winter, so he wanted to move to the countryside. It was unexpected and I only had a week to find a new host family. I asked my friend Danielle if I could live with her until I found a new home. That's how I met the Dirksen family, my fifth family.

The Dirksen family had three kids. They were all different. Danielle liked bitter black coffee, Christian liked energy drinks, and Becca liked sweet lemon tea. Dawn, the host mom didn't like winter, and Mark, the host dad, didn't like summer. After dinner, we would all play Wii Sports together. I was the king of bowling, and Dawn was the queen of tennis. I don't remember a single time that they argued about the games. Afterward, we would gather in the living room and Danielle would play the piano while the rest of us sang hymns.

Of course, those 28 months were too short to fully understand all five families, but I learned from and was shaped by each of them. By teaching me English, nine year-old Cody taught me the importance of being able to learn from anyone; the Martinez family showed me the value of spending time together as a family; the Struiksma family taught me to reserve judgment about divorced women and adopted children; Mrs. Ortiz taught me the value of discipline and the Dirksen family taught me the importance of appreciating one another's different qualities.

Getting along with other people is necessary for anyone and living with five families has made me more sensitive to others' needs: I have learned how to recognize when someone needs to talk, when I should give advice and when to simply listen, and when someone needs to be left alone; in the process, I have become much more adaptable. I'm ready to change, learn, and be shaped by my future families.

It's this final value, being "adaptable," that connects ALL his experiences with the five families, and it's a value he'll carry on to his future families—in college and beyond. Final boom.

Margin annotations:

Hint 5.

All along he was weaving in these little tiny lessons that he learned. It's satisfying to reveal the connection here at the end. But wait, he's not finished.

So what has all this been leading up to?

Let the series of explosions in your mind begin...Boom: Payoff/Lesson 1.

Boom: Payoff/ Lesson 2.

Boom: Payoff/ Lesson 3.

Boom: Payoff/ Lesson 4.

Boom: Payoff/ Lesson 5.

Such a beautiful last line. Don't you just wanna hug him?

How can you use this technique for your essay?

You can't.

I'm kidding again. You actually can. The key is this... Wait, before I tell you, here's a word of warning:

Don't try to preplan this too much.

The author of the "Five Families" essay was able to discover this approach only *after* he'd written some really detailed paragraphs about the experience of living with these families. By trying to find an interesting way to connect the five families, he discovered there were lessons buried in a couple of the family descriptions, and he thought he might be able to set up some lessons in the other family paragraphs and then reveal all the lessons at the end. Again, it was important that his "hints" (the lessons) were clear enough for us to remember, but not so obvious that it'd be predictable where he was headed with the essay while we were reading it. How did he do this? On a basic level, he chose to "show" (set up) his lessons in the first few paragraphs, and then chose to "tell" all the lessons at the end. And I just want to reiterate that this was *discovered* and not preplanned.

Wait, so how did the author do this?

Here's a breakdown:

LEVEL 1.0

First, he found some interesting things to talk about. Essentially, he found a variety of interesting experiences to describe. So he had an initial framing device: *I'm going to give a variety of details about my experiences with these five families.* But then...

LEVEL 2.0

He found *a deeper way that they were all connected.* How? He realized that he "learned from and was shaped by each of [these families]" (see next to last paragraph). Nice! This connected them all. But he didn't stop there.

LEVEL 3.0

He found yet *another* way they were all connected. How? All of them taught him the value of...adaptability (see last paragraph). Great. So it's like Level 2.0 drew out something the families had in common (he learned a lesson from each), and Level 3.0 identified a value he gained from living with all of them (adaptability).

Together, these threads give the essay a feeling of inevitability, as though the author knew where he was taking us the whole time (even though, at first, he didn't). And it's surprising because we didn't necessarily think that all the families were going to connect in any particular way—we certainly didn't see there was a lesson buried in each paragraph as we were reading—and we didn't know they would all be tied together with a common value.

That's what makes it surprising *and* inevitable—we had some sense that the paragraphs probably *would* connect, but as we read through the essay, we didn't really know *how*.

Final Words on This Technique

Again, don't try to preplan too much. Why?

1. Preplanning can get really frustrating if you're trying to make this structure work, but you find the events of your life simply don't work with this structure. It can feel forced. So don't force it. Preplanning can actually prevent or postpone you from finding a structure and a flow that will work for *your* life story.
2. It can end up sounding pretty mechanical and obvious if you're too aware of your ending when you begin your story. In other words, sometimes if you're trying to Set Up Something, the "surprise" ending won't be very surprising because the Buried Hints won't be sufficiently buried. They may all be kind of

obvious and on-the-surface, and there won't be enough interesting stuff around the hints to distract us from what you're doing. (Remember, this is like a magic trick, and we need a misdirect—something shiny or pretty to focus on while the magic is happening behind the scenes.)

Instead, write interesting paragraphs with interesting details that correspond to the *original* focusing lens. Let me clarify what I mean by that. In the "Five Families" essay, the author began by writing some nice details about each family. So the reader is able to get pulled into *that* and perhaps be lulled into thinking that maybe this is as deep as it goes.

Then: BAM—an aha moment for the reader. And you want to know how to get the most aha into your aha moment? If you discover it yourself along the way. It takes patience and a trust of the process (or openness to the possibility that you may not actually discover a deeper connection), but chances are the thing you discover as you write will be much more interesting than the thing you preplan. Let me say that again, and make it look like an epic quote, so you remember it:

> "The connections that you discover along the way will be much more interesting than those you try to plan."
>
> —ME

ADVANCED TECHNIQUE 5: MAKE IT NEW

Degree of difficulty: 8.0–10.0★ (depends on what you're making new)

> "Make it new."
>
> —EZRA POUND

I know it seems redundant to put a quote with the exact same words as the technique, but doing so gives this final point *legitimacy*. Because Ezra Pound said this, too. And Ezra Pound is *legit*.

What does it mean to "make it new"?

For years, filmmakers have been taking familiar stories and recontextualizing them.

Some examples include:

- *Apocalypse Now*: Joseph Conrad's *Heart of Darkness* set during the Vietnam War
- *O Brother, Where Art Thou?*: Homer's *Odyssey* adapted to the 1930s American South
- The updated *Annie* musical, produced by Jay Z and Will Smith and starring Quvenzhané Wallis, which is set in modern-day New York City and is a remake of the original *Annie* musical that was based on the *Little Orphan Annie* comic strip.

You can do this with your essay, too.

Which essay prompts will this technique work best with?

I think it works best for creative, open-ended supplemental essay prompts such as:

- the University of Chicago "Create your own prompt" essay, or
- any school that asks, "What else would you like us to know about you?" (Note that some schools, in particular a few Ivies, ask this at the very end of the application. This is your opportunity to show one more side of yourself. Don't pass up this chance!)

This can also definitely work for your main essay, but it's just a bit more difficult to pull off—thus the "advanced technique" label.

What "it" should you be making new?

That's up to you. Want some options? Take a look at Greek, Roman, Jewish, Christian, or Islamic stories and myths. Or consider remaking a fairy tale (What's the *real* Cinderella story?), a holiday origin story (How did Christmas *really* begin?), or even doing an alternate take on an old joke (Why do firemen actually wear red suspenders?).

This last option—a new take on an old joke—is exactly what this next student does. And note that everything under the title is her writing.

"WHY DID THE CHICKEN CROSS THE ROAD?"

Note to reader: I plan to double major in biochemistry and English and my main essay explains my passion for the former; here is a writing sample that illustrates my enthusiasm for the latter.

In my AP Literature class, my teacher posed a question to which students had to write a creative response. My response is framed around the ideas of Plato's "Allegory of the Cave."

Q: Why did the chicken cross the road?

A: A manicured green field of grass blades cut to perfectly matched lengths; a blue expanse ornamented with puffy cotton clouds; an immaculately painted red barn centered exactly at the top of a hill—the chicken gazes contentedly at his picturesque world. Within an area surrounded by a shiny silver fence, he looks around at his friends: roosters pecking at a feast of grains and hens lounging on luxurious cushions of hay. As the nice man in a plaid shirt and blue jeans collects the hens' eggs, the chicken feels an overwhelming sense of indebtedness to him for providing this idyllic lifestyle.

On a day as pristine as all the others, the chicken is happily eating his lunchtime meal as the nice man carefully gathers the smooth white eggs when it notices that the man has left one behind. Strangely located at the empty end of the metal enclosure, highlighted by the bright yellow sun, the white egg appears to the chicken different from the rest. The chicken moves towards the light to tacitly inform the man of his mistake. But then the chicken notices a jagged gray line on the otherwise flawless egg. Hypnotized and appalled, the chicken watches as the line turns into a crack and a small beak attached to a fuzzy yellow head pokes out. Suddenly a shadow descends over the chicken and the nice man snatches the egg—the baby chick— and stomps off.

The chicken—confused, betrayed, disturbed—slowly lifts its eyes from the now empty ground. For the first time, it looks past the silver fence of the cage and notices an unkempt sweep of colossal brown and green grasses opposite its impeccably crafted surroundings. Cautiously, it inches closer to the barrier, farther from the unbelievable perfection of the farm, and discovers a wide sea of black gravel. Stained with gray stones and marked with yellow lines, it separates the chicken from the opposite field.

The curious chicken quickly shuffles to Mother Hen, who has just settled on to her throne of hay and is closing her eyes. He is sure that the always composed and compassionate chicken will help him make sense of what he's just seen.

"Mother Hen, Mother Hen! I-I just saw one of those eggs, cracking, and there was a small yellow bird inside. It was a baby. Are those eggs that the nice man takes away babies? And that black ground! What is it?" the chicken blurts out.

Her eyes flick open. "BOK BOK! Don't you ever dare speak of what you have seen again," Mother Hen snaps in a low and violent whisper, "or all of this will be taken away." Closing her eyes again, she dismisses the chicken.

Frozen in disbelief, the chicken tries to make sense of her

harsh words. It replays the incident in its head. "All the food, the nice soft hay, the flawless red barn—maybe all of this isn't worth giving up. Maybe Mother Hen is right. She just wants to protect me from losing it all." The chicken replays the incident again. "But it was a baby. What if it was hers? She still wouldn't care. She's being selfish; all she cares about is this perfect life." A final replay, and the chicken realizes and accepts that Mother Hen knows, has known, that the man is doing something wrong; yet she has yielded to the cruelty for her own comfort. A fissure in the chicken's unawareness, a plan begins to hatch. The chicken knows it must escape; it has to get to the other side.

"That man in the plaid shirt is stealing the eggs from their mothers again," the chicken thinks the next day as he unlocks the cage. Then the man reaches into the wooden coop, his back to the entrance. "Now!" At its own cue, the chicken scurries towards the opening and exits unseen. With a backwards glance at his friends, the chicken feels a profound sadness and pity for their ignorance. It wants to urge them to open their eyes, to see what they are sacrificing for materialistic pleasures, but he knows they will not surrender the false reality. Alone, the chicken dashes away.

The chicken stands at the line between green grass and black gravel. As it prepares to take its first step into the unknown, a monstrous vehicle with 18 wheels made of metal whizzes by, leaving behind a trail of gray exhaust. Once it regains its breath, it moves a few inches onto the asphalt. Three more speeding trucks stop its chicken heart.

"I can't do this," it says to itself. "These monsters are a sign. They're telling me to go back. Besides, a few lost chicks aren't so bad. The man's not that evil. He gives us food, and a home." But the chicken dismisses the cowardly voice in its head, reminding itself of the injustice back in the deceptively charming prison. Over the next several hours, it learns to strategically position itself so that it is in line with the empty space between the tires of passing trucks. It reaches the yellow dashes. A black blanket gradually pushes away the glowing sun and replaces it with diamond stars and a glowing crescent. It reaches the untouched field.

With a deep breath, the chicken steps into the swathe, a world of tall beige grass made brown by the darkness. Unsure of what it may discover, it determines to simply walk straight through the brush, out on to the other side. For what seems like forever, it continues forward, as the black sky turns to purple, then blue, then pink. Just as the chicken begins to regret its journey, the grass gives way to a vast landscape of trees, bushes, flowers—heterogeneous and variable, but nonetheless perfect. In a nearby tree, the chicken spots two adult birds tending to a nest of babies—a natural dynamic of individuals unaltered by corrupt influence.

And then it dawns on him. It has escaped from a contrived and perverted domain as well as its own unawareness; it has arrived in a place where the pure order of the world reigns.

"I know the truth now," it thinks to himself as the sun rises. "But here, in Nature, it is of no use. Back home, I need to try to foster awareness among my friends, share this understanding with them. Otherwise, I am as cruel as the man in the plaid shirt, taking away the opportunity to overcome ignorance."

I must return now, thought the chicken. *I have to get to the other side.*

Analysis of "Why Did the Chicken Cross the Road?"

Note to reader: I plan to double major in biochemistry and English and my main essay explains my passion for the former; here is a writing sample that illustrates my enthusi-asm for the latter.

Love the context.

In my AP Literature class, my teacher posed a question to which students had to write a creative response. My response is framed around the ideas of Plato's "Allegory of the Cave."

Otherwise we might wonder, "What the heck is she talking about?"

Q: Why did the chicken cross the road?

A: A manicured green field of grass blades cut to perfectly matched lengths; a blue expanse ornamented with puffy cotton clouds; an immaculately painted red barn centered exactly at the top of a hill—the chicken gazes contentedly at his pictur-esque world. Within an area surrounded by a shiny silver fence, he looks around at his friends: roosters pecking at a feast of grains and hens lounging on luxurious cushions of hay. As the nice man in a plaid shirt and blue jeans collects the hens' eggs, the chicken feels an overwhelming sense of indebtedness to him for providing this idyllic lifestyle.

She debated for a week on whether or not to include this note, and ultimately she wanted to make sure the reader really got it. I think she made the right choice.

Status quo: Note the great details.

On a day as pristine as all the others, the chicken is happily eating his lunchtime meal as the nice man carefully gathers the smooth white eggs when it notices that the man has left one behind. Strangely located at the empty end of the metal enclosure, highlighted by the bright yellow sun, the white egg appears to the chicken different from the rest. The chicken moves towards the light to tacitly inform the man of his mistake. But then the chicken notices a jagged gray line on the otherwise flawless egg. Hypnotized and appalled, the chicken watches as the line turns into a crack and a small beak attached to a fuzzy yellow head pokes out. Suddenly a shadow descends over the chicken and the nice man snatches the egg—the baby chick—and stomps off.

Setup for raising of the stakes.

The chicken—confused, betrayed, disturbed—slowly lifts its eyes from the now empty ground. For the first time, it looks past the silver fence of the cage and notices an unkempt sweep of colossal brown and green grasses opposite its impeccably

Inciting incident.

crafted surroundings. Cautiously, it inches closer to the barrier, farther from the unbelievable perfection of the farm, and discovers a wide sea of black gravel. Stained with gray stones and marked with yellow lines, it separates the chicken from the opposite field.

The curious chicken quickly shuffles to Mother Hen, who has just settled on to her throne of hay and is closing her eyes. He is sure that the always composed and compassionate chicken will help him make sense of what he's just seen.

"Mother Hen, Mother Hen! I-I just saw one of those eggs, cracking, and there was a small yellow bird inside. It was a baby. Are those eggs that the nice man takes away babies? And that black ground! What is it?" the chicken blurts out.

I love that the chicken can talk.

Her eyes flick open. "BOK BOK! Don't you ever dare speak of what you have seen again," Mother Hen snaps in a low and violent whisper, "or all of this will be taken away." Closing her eyes again, she dismisses the chicken.

Raise the stakes.

Frozen in disbelief, the chicken tries to make sense of her harsh words. It replays the incident in its head. "All the food, the nice soft hay, the flawless red barn—maybe all of this isn't worth giving up. Maybe Mother Hen is right. She just wants to protect me from losing it all." The chicken replays the incident again. "But it was a baby. What if it was hers? She still wouldn't care. She's being selfish; all she cares about is this perfect life." A final replay, and the chicken realizes and accepts that Mother Hen knows, has known, that the man is doing something wrong; yet she has yielded to the cruelty for her own comfort. A fissure in the chicken's unawareness, a plan begins to hatch. The chicken knows it must escape; it has to get to the other side.

Reiterating the raising of the stakes (just to make sure we get it).

The question of the essay—Why did the chicken cross the road?—is answered here.

"That man in the plaid shirt is stealing the eggs from their mothers again," the chicken thinks the next day as he unlocks the cage. Then the man reaches into the wooden coop, his back

End of essay? No way. Why? Because now we're waiting to find out how.

to the entrance. "Now!" At its own cue, the chicken scurries towards the opening and exits unseen. With a backwards glance at his friends, the chicken feels a profound sadness and pity for their ignorance. It wants to urge them to open their eyes, to see what they are sacrificing for materialistic pleasures, but he knows they will not surrender the false reality. Alone, the chicken dashes away.

Raise the stakes; also a setup for the ending.

The chicken stands at the line between green grass and black gravel. As it prepares to take its first step into the unknown, a monstrous vehicle with 18 wheels made of metal whizzes by, leaving behind a trail of gray exhaust. Once it regains its breath, it moves a few inches onto the asphalt. Three more speeding trucks stop its chicken heart.

Raise the stakes.

Funny. Intelligent humor = great.

"I can't do this," it says to itself. "These monsters are a sign. They're telling me to go back. Besides, a few lost chicks aren't so bad. The man's not that evil. He gives us food, and a home."

Raise the stakes: The chicken is going to give up!

But the chicken dismisses the cowardly voice in its head, reminding itself of the injustice back in the deceptively charming prison. Over the next several hours, it learns to strategically position itself so that it is in line with the empty space between the tires of passing trucks. It reaches the yellow dashes. A black blanket gradually pushes away the glowing sun and replaces it with diamond stars and a glowing crescent. It reaches the untouched field.

In film terms, this is the end of the climax. Chicken has arrived! We sigh. Next is the denouement.

With a deep breath, the chicken steps into the swathe, a world of tall beige grass made brown by the darkness. Unsure of what it may discover, it determines to simply walk straight through the brush, out on to the other side. For what seems like forever, it continues forward, as the black sky turns to purple, then blue, then pink. Just as the chicken begins to regret its journey, the grass gives way to a vast landscape of trees, bushes, flowers—heterogeneous and variable, but nonetheless perfect. In a nearby tree, the chicken spots two adult birds tending to

New status quo.

a nest of babies—a natural dynamic of individuals unaltered by corrupt influence.

And then it dawns on him. It has escaped from a contrived and perverted domain as well as its own unawareness; it has arrived in a place where the pure order of the world reigns.

"I know the truth now," it thinks to himself as the sun rises. "But here, in Nature, it is of no use. Back home, I need to try to foster awareness among my friends, share this understanding with them. Otherwise, I am as cruel as the man in the plaid shirt, taking away the opportunity to overcome ignorance.

I must return now, thought the chicken. *I have to get to the other side.*

Amazing final line. It's inevitable (because it references the familiar joke), but it's surprising because you probably thought the "Why did the chicken cross the road" was referring to the first time the chicken crosses the road in the essay, BUT IT'S ACTUALLY ABOUT CROSSING BACK. And that wasn't easy to predict. It also gives the essay a kind of circularity (it's a payoff!), plus it sets up beautifully for her sequel.

Here's one more "make it new" example:

"ROCK, PAPER, SCISSORS"
Written for the University of Chicago prompt, which asked applicants to create their own prompt

Prompt:

Dear Christian,

The admissions staff at the University of Chicago would like to inform you that your application has been "put on the line." We have one spot left and can't decide if we should admit you or another equally qualified applicant. To resolve the matter, please choose one of the following:

Rock, paper, or scissors.

You will be notified of our decision shortly.

Response:

Rock beats scissors, scissors beats paper, and paper beats rock. Wait... paper beats rock? Since when has a sheet of loose leaf paper ever defeated a solid block of granite? Do we assume that the paper wraps around the rock, smothering the rock into submission? When exposed to paper, is rock somehow immobilized, unable to fulfill its primary function of smashing scissors? What constitutes defeat between two inanimate objects?

Maybe it's all a metaphor for larger ideals. Perhaps paper is rooted in the symbolism of diplomacy while rock suggests coercion. But does compromise necessarily trump brute force? And where do scissors lie in this chain of symbolism?

I guess the reasoning behind this game has a lot to do with context. If we are to rationalize the logic behind this game, we have to assume some kind of narrative, an instance in which paper might beat rock. Unfortunately, I can't argue for a convincing one.

As with rock-paper-scissors, we often cut our narratives short to make the games we play easier, ignoring the intricate assumptions that keep the game running smoothly. Like rock-paper-scissors, we tend to accept something not because it's true, but because it's the convenient route to getting things accomplished. We accept incomplete narratives when they serve us well, overlooking their logical gaps. Other times, we exaggerate even the smallest defects and uncertainties in narratives we don't want to deal with. In a world where we know very little about the nature of "Truth," it's very easy—and tempting—to construct stories around truth claims that unfairly legitimize or delegitimize the games we play.

Or maybe I'm just making a big deal out of nothing...

Fine. I'll stop with the semantics and play your game.

But who actually wants to play a game of rock-paper-scissors? After all, isn't it just a game of random luck, requiring zero skill and talent? That's no way to admit someone!

Wrong.

Studies have shown that there are winning strategies to rock-paper-scissors by making critical assumptions about those we play against before the round has even started. Douglas Walker, host of the Rock-Paper-Scissors World Championships (didn't know that existed either), conducted research indicating that males will use rock as their opening move 50% of the time, a gesture Walker believes is due to rock's symbolic association with strength and force. In this sense, the seemingly innocuous game of rock-paper-scissors has revealed something quite discomforting about gender-related dispositions in our society. Why did so many males think that brute strength was the best option? If social standards have subliminally influenced the way males and females play rock-paper-scissors, than [sic] what is to prevent such biases from skewing more important decisions? Should your decision to go to war or to feed the hungry depend on your gender, race, creed, etc?

Perhaps the narratives I spoke of earlier, the stories I mistakenly labeled as "semantics," carry real weight in our everyday decisions. In the case of Walker's study, men unconsciously created an irrational narrative around an abstract rock. We all tell slightly different narratives when we independently consider notions ranging from rocks to war to existence. It is ultimately the unconscious gaps in these narratives that are responsible for many of the man-made problems this world faces. In order for the "life of the mind" to be a worthwhile endeavor, we must challenge the unconscious narratives we attach to the larger games we play—the truths we tell (or don't tell), the lessons we learn (or haven't really learned), the people we meet (or haven't truly met).

But even after all of this, we still don't completely understand the narrative behind rock-paper-scissors.

I guess it all comes down to who actually made this silly game in the first place… I'd like to think it was some snotty 3rd grader, but then again, that's just another incomplete narrative.

Just to reiterate: the topic of this essay (and the "Why Did the Chicken Cross the Road?" essay) may not be ideal topics for a main personal statement. Why? I'm not sure I learn a ton about the student's world or dreams and aspirations from these—or, to put it another way, I prefer personal statements that are a little more, well, personal. How do you get personal? I think vulnerability is the key (something I discuss in more depth on page 183 in "How to Make Sure Your Essay Is Doing Its Job"), and I like to be able to name a greater number and variety of a student's values by the end of the essay than I can name with these. But both of these make great supplemental essays (and along with the "Santur" essay, they are the only supplemental essays in this book) because they demonstrate intelligence, writing ability, and tons of intellectual curiosity, all of which colleges appreciate. Personally, I love this essay, not just because it's so darn fun to read, but also because (get this) it was a first draft. I know this because I was present for the moment when, days before the deadline, the author landed on the idea. I received an email less than twenty-four hours later with this essay. I read it on my phone and wrote back the words "Nice job."

WHAT MAKES AN ESSAY AMAZING

Following are two essays that I find to be, well, amazing. Read them first, without analysis, and then we'll look at four elements that make them amazing.

This first essay was originally written for a "topic of your choice" prompt, but it could work for any number of prompts. It's more than 1,000 words, but I'm including it as is, since this was how the author submitted it.

"I SHOT MY BROTHER"

From page 54 of the maroon notebook sitting on my mahogany desk:

Then Cain said to the Lord, "My punishment is greater than I can bear. I shall be a fugitive and a wanderer on the earth and whoever finds me will kill me."—Genesis 4:13

Here is a secret that no one in my family knows: I shot my brother when I was six. Luckily, it was [with] a BB gun. But to this day, my older brother Jonathan does not know who shot him. And I have finally promised myself to confess this eleven year old secret to him after I write this essay.

The truth is, I was always jealous of my brother. Our grandparents, with whom we lived as children in Daegu, a rural city in South Korea, showered my brother with endless accolades: he was bright, athletic, and charismatic.

"Why can't you be more like Jon?" my grandmother used to nag, pointing at me with a carrot stick. To me, Jon was just cocky. He would scoff at me when he would beat me in basketball, and when he brought home his painting of Bambi with the teacher's sticker "Awesome!" on top, he would make several copies of it and showcase them on the refrigerator door. But I retreated to my desk where a pile of "Please draw this again and bring it to me tomorrow" papers lay, desperate for immediate treatment. Later, I even refused to attend the same elementary school and wouldn't even eat meals with him.

Deep down I knew I had to get the chip off my shoulder. But I didn't know how.

That is, until March 11th, 2001.

That day around six o'clock, juvenile combatants appeared in Kyung Mountain for their weekly battle, with cheeks smeared in mud and empty BB guns in their hands. The Korean War game was simple: to kill your opponent you had to shout "pow!" before he did. Once we situated ourselves, our captain blew the pinkie whistle and the war began. My friend Min-young and I hid behind a willow tree, eagerly awaiting our orders.

Beside us, our comrades were dying, each falling to the ground crying in "agony," their hands clasping their "wounds." Suddenly a wish for heroism surged within me: I grabbed Min-young's arms and rushed towards the enemies' headquarters, disobeying our orders to remain sentry duty. To tip the tide of the war, I had to kill their captain. We infiltrated the enemy lines, narrowly dodging each attack. We then cleared the pillars of asparagus ferns until the Captain's lair came into view. I quickly pulled my clueless friend back into the bush.

Hearing us, the alarmed captain turned around: It was my brother.

He saw Min-young's right arm sticking out from the bush and hurled a "grenade," (a rock), bruising his arm.

"That's not fair!" I roared in the loudest and most unrecognizable voice I could manage.

Startled, the Captain and his generals abandoned their post. Vengeance replaced my wish for heroism and I took off after the fleeing perpetrator. Streams of sweat ran down my face and I pursued him for several minutes until suddenly I was arrested by a small, yellow sign that read in Korean: DO NOT TRESPASS: Boar Traps Ahead. (Two summers ago, my five year old cousin, who insisted on joining the ranks, had wandered off-course during the battle; we found him at the bottom of a 20 ft deep pit with a deep gash in his forehead and shirt soaked in blood.) "Hey, stop!" I shouted, heart pounding. "STOP!"

My mind froze. My eyes just gazed at the fleeing object; what should I do?

I looked on as my shivering hand reached for the canister of BBs. The next second, I heard two shots followed by a cry. I opened my eyes just enough to see two village men carrying my brother away from the warning sign. I turned around, hurled my BB gun into the nearby Kyung Creek and ran home as fast as I could.

***

Days passed. My brother and I did not talk about the incident.

'Maybe he knew it was me,' I thought in fear as I tried to eavesdrop on his conversation with grandpa one day. When the door suddenly opened, I blurted, "Is anything wrong?"

"Nothing," he said pushing past me, "Just a rough sleep."

But in the next few weeks, something was happening inside me.

All the jealousy and anger I'd once felt had been replaced by a new feeling: guilt.

That night when my brother was gone I went to a local store and bought a piece of chocolate taffy, his favorite. I returned home and placed it on my brother's bed with a note attached: "Love, Grandma."

Several days later, I secretly went into his room and folded his unkempt pajamas.

Then, other things began to change. We began sharing clothes (something we had never done), started watching Pokémon episodes together, and then, on his ninth birthday, I did something with Jon that I hadn't done in six years: I ate dinner with him. I even ate fishcakes, which he loved but I hated. And I didn't complain.

Today, my brother is one of my closest friends. Every week I accompany him to Carlson Hospital where he receives treatment for his obsessive compulsive disorder and schizophrenia.

While in the waiting room, we play a noisy game of Zenga, comment on the Lakers' performance or listen to the radio on the registrar's desk.

Then, the door to the doctor's office opens.

"Jonathan Lee, please come in."

I tap his shoulder and whisper, "Rock it, bro."

After he leaves, I take out my notebook and begin writing where I left off.

Beside me, the receptionist's fingers hover over the radio in search of a new station, eventually settling on one. I hear LeAnn Rimes singing "Amazing Grace." Her voice slowly rises over the noise of the bustling room.

"'Twas Grace that taught my heart to fear. And Grace, my fears relieved…"

Smiling, I open Jon's Jansport backpack and neatly place this essay inside and a chocolate taffy with a note attached.

Twenty minutes have passed when the door abruptly opens.

"Guess what the doctor just said?" my brother cries, unable to hide his exhilaration.

I look up and I smile too.

This next essay was originally written for a prompt that read, "Evaluate a significant experience, risk, achievement, or ethical dilemma you have faced and its impact on you."

"DYING BIRD"

Smeared blood, shredded feathers. Clearly, the bird was dead. But wait, the slight fluctuation of its chest, the slow blinking of its shiny black eyes. No, it was alive.

I had been typing an English essay when I heard my cat's loud meows and the flutter of wings. I had turned slightly at the noise and had found the barely breathing bird in front of me.

The shock came first. Mind racing, heart beating faster, blood draining from my face. I instinctively reached out my hand to hold it, like a long-lost keepsake from my youth. But then I remembered that birds had life, flesh, blood.

Death. Dare I say it out loud? Here, in my own home?

Within seconds, my reflexes kicked in. Get over the shock. Gloves, napkins, towels. Band-aid? How does one heal a bird? I rummaged through the house, keeping a wary eye on my cat. Donning yellow rubber gloves, I tentatively picked up the bird. Never mind the cat's hissing and protesting scratches, you need to save the bird. You need to ease its pain.

But my mind was blank. I stroked the bird with a paper towel to clear away the blood, see the wound. The wings were crumpled, the feet mangled. A large gash extended close to its jugular rendering its breathing shallow, unsteady. The rising and falling of its small breast slowed. Was the bird dying? No, please, not yet.

Why was this feeling so familiar, so tangible?

Oh. Yes. The long drive, the green hills, the white church, the funeral. The Chinese mass, the resounding amens, the flower arrangements. Me, crying silently, huddled in the corner. The Hsieh family huddled around the casket. Apologies. So many apologies. Finally, the body lowered to rest. The body. Kari Hsieh. Still familiar, still tangible.

Hugging Mrs. Hsieh, I was a ghost, a statue. My brain and my body competed. Emotion wrestled with fact. Kari Hsieh, aged 17, my friend of four years, had died in the Chatsworth Metrolink Crash on Sep. 12, 2008. Kari was dead, I thought. Dead.

But I could still save the bird.

My frantic actions heightened my senses, mobilized my spirit. Cupping the bird, I ran outside, hoping the cool air outdoors would suture every wound, cause the bird to miraculously fly away. Yet there lay the bird in my hands, still gasping, still dying. Bird, human, human, bird. What was the difference? Both were the same. Mortal.

But couldn't I do something? Hold the bird longer, de-claw the cat? I wanted to go to my bedroom, confine myself to tears, replay my memories, never come out.

The bird's warmth faded away. Its heartbeat slowed along with its breath. For a long time, I stared thoughtlessly at it, so still in my hands.

Slowly, I dug a small hole in the black earth. As it disappeared under handfuls of dirt, my own heart grew stronger, my own breath more steady.

The wind, the sky, the dampness of the soil on my hands whispered to me, "The bird is dead. Kari has passed. But you are alive." My breath, my heartbeat, my sweat sighed back, "I am alive. I am alive. I am alive."

Four Qualities of an Amazing Essay

Before I discuss the four qualities, here's an important qualifier:

When I share the two essays you just read in my workshops, readers tend to fall into two camps. Some say:

1. "Great story! But NOT a great college essay."

While others say:

2. "Great story AND a great college essay!"

Those in the first camp argue that the authors do not sufficiently demonstrate the qualities, skills, and values that they would bring to a college campus—in short, readers feel they don't really get a sense of who the student is.

Those in the second camp note that the authors' writing ability, attention to detail, and emotional intelligence are enough to let them know they'd contribute a lot to a college.

There is, of course, no right answer.

I see both sides. To be honest, I worked with these students several years ago. If I were to work with them today, I think I'd actually advise different topics, or different treatments of the topics, simply because I've become more conservative in how I advise students and, frankly, I think these essays are risky. (And by "conservative," I mean that I tend to advise students according to the criteria outlined in "How to Make Sure Your Essay Is Doing Its Job" on page 183, which these essays may or may not pass.)

With that said, my goal here is not to tell you what you must do, but instead to offer you creative options and let you make up your own mind. Whether or not the two essays would make great essays, I believe they are great pieces of writing and have a lot to teach us. So let's get to it!

A great story has two parts: a narrative that engages, often through a series of images, and an insight that illuminates something about the images and essentially answers "so what?" Although I've read a lot of essays, the two you've just read have two of the most interesting narrative and "so what" combinations I've ever seen. As I looked at them side-by-side, I realized they had a few things in common, traits that I now refer to as my "Four Qualities of an Amazing Essay."

Here are four qualities that these essays share:

1. The story is unusual in either content, structure, or both.
2. The story has at least one "wow" moment.
3. The ending is both surprising and inevitable.
4. The ending makes the reader do a little bit of work.

Note that these are not the *only* qualities of an amazing essay, but they are qualities that these amazing essays share.

Analysis of "I Shot My Brother"

1. Unusual elements

a. Unusual content (the "what"): How many people shoot their brother? Beyond that, how many shoot their brother *in order to save his life?* Not many.

b. Unusual structure (the "how"): Nonchronological order of events (essay begins with the ending). Includes cinematic time jumps.

c. Unusual style (the "how"): Great dialogue. Realistic characters. Memorable visual details. One of the best essay openings I have ever read.

2. The "wow" moment

a. The moment he has to shoot his brother in order to save his life.

b. Double wow: He's also been looking to get back at his brother, so shooting him is both an "I love you" and "I hate you" moment.

c. Triple wow: The moment of violence ends up being the catalyst for ultimately bringing them together.

3. The ending is both surprising and inevitable

a. Surprising: No way will these two reconcile.

b. Inevitable: Of course they'll reconcile.

c. Also surprising: Even if we suspected they would reconcile, we didn't expect it would happen in this way.

4. The ending makes the reader do a little bit of work

Look at that ending again—what does it mean?

> Smiling, I open Jon's Jansport backpack and neatly place this essay inside and a chocolate taffy with a note attached.

> Twenty minutes have passed when the door abruptly opens.
> "Guess what the doctor just said?" my brother cries, unable
> to hide his exhilaration.
> I look up and I smile too.

I won't spell it out. Just think about where his relationship with his brother was at the start of the story (status quo) and think about where it is now (new status quo).

Analysis of "Dying Bird"
1. Unusual elements

a. Unusual content (the "what"): Who gets the chance to save a dying bird? Who makes a connection to a friend while the bird is dying? Not many people.
b. Unusual structure (the "how"): The nonchronological opening— she starts with an arresting image, then does a flashback to fill us in on the context.
c. Unusual style (the "how"): The clipped style of the writing. Like a series of snapshots or a film with very quick takes.

2. The "wow" moment

a. The moment when she realizes that her struggle to let the bird go parallels her struggle to let her friend go. It's not explicit, so you have to look for it. But it's there.

3. The ending is both surprising and inevitable

a. Why surprising? We didn't expect her to make peace with the bird's death or her friend's.
b. Why inevitable? Once we think about it, of course she'd have to accept the bird's death and her friend's.

4. The ending makes the reader do a little bit of work

Look at that ending again—what does it mean?

> The wind, the sky, the dampness of the soil on my hands
> whispered to me, "The bird is dead. Kari has passed. But you
> are alive." My breath, my heartbeat, my sweat sighed back, "I
> am alive. I am alive. I am alive."

It's subtle, what I would call a poetic ending, and I'll define "poetic" in this way—it leaves something unaccounted for. To get the meaning, you have to think about it a little, and different readers may have different interpretations. Note that it's easy to do this poorly and hard to do this well. In terms of what the ending to this essay means, I won't ruin it by trying to explain it. I'll let you decide for yourself.

Also, both of these essays end with some kind of redemption. I'm not saying that's required for an amazing essay, but I think it's part of what makes my heart swell each time I read them.

Again, these are not the *only* qualities of an amazing essay, nor are they required to make your essay amazing. These are simply qualities that I have observed in two essays that I find amazing. Incorporating these concepts can help you create a piece of writing that will amaze the reader and may even be considered by some to be a work of art.

But many students haven't experienced crazy, unusual circumstances, and some students aren't necessarily looking to create a piece of art.

Is it still possible to write an excellent college essay despite the fact that you didn't shoot your brother when you were six or see a bird die and recognize it as a metaphor for your friend's death?

Of course it is. The next chapter explains how.

CHAPTER EIGHT

How to Make Sure Your Essay Is Doing Its Job

IT'S STILL POSSIBLE TO WRITE a great college essay even if you haven't undergone crazy, unusual circumstances. In fact, maybe you just want to make sure your essay is doing its job. And what is its job? Well, think about it a second. The colleges you apply to will have a record of your grades, test scores, and extracurricular activities. So clearly your essay should show something that hasn't already been made evident. But that's kind of an obvious answer. Your essay might also contextualize or explain any red flags on your application (like bad grades) so that you're not judged too harshly. But that shouldn't be the main point of your essay. I believe the main point of your essay—actually, hang on, let me say this in bold and italics:

The aim of your college essay is to illustrate that you will make valuable contributions in college and beyond.

Why? Because college admissions offices are putting together a team...no, wait, they're hosting a dinner party and there's just one seat left...no, actually they're inviting you into their family—okay, enough analogies, you get the point. In short, colleges want to know how you'd contribute to life on campus. And they want to imagine you'll do amazing things once you graduate.

How do you illustrate that you will make valuable contributions in college and beyond? I believe it's by demonstrating these qualities:

1. Core values (a.k.a. *information*)
2. Vulnerability
3. "So what" moments (a.k.a. *important and interesting connections*)

If you work to incorporate all these things into your essay over a series of drafts, and you work to tell a story that is both compelling and succinct, you will end up with something called:

4. Craft

Here's why I believe each of these qualities is important:

1. **Core values (a.k.a. information)**: The best essays provide valuable information about the author. And I'm not talking about trivial facts—your favorite basketball team, for example, or whether you prefer brown or green M&M's—I'm talking about four to five values that are essential to who you are.
2. **Vulnerability**: The best essays offer more than superficial information; they hit you in the gut and make you feel things— the ups and downs, the passions and frustrations of the author.
3. **"So what" moments (a.k.a. important and interesting connections)**: "The best way for me to tell if a student is college-ready," says Kati Sweaney of Reed College, "is if the student can answer 'So what?' in the essay." I agree.

And I believe it's important to do so several times throughout the essay.

4. **Craft**: The best essays demonstrate a series of carefully considered choices. And in the best essays, every word counts.

How can you tell if your essay is great?

Turn the page and take The Great College Essay Test.

THE GREAT COLLEGE ESSAY TEST

Is your essay great? The criteria below will help you decide. And, as in the "Four Qualities of an Amazing Essay" section, these are not the *only* qualities of a great essay—these are just a few qualities that I have observed in essays that I find to be great.

How might you use these criteria? Read your essay aloud, or have someone else read it aloud. Then ask these questions:

1. Core values (a.k.a. information)
   → Can you name at least four to five of the author's core values?
   → Do you detect a variety of values, or do the values repeat?
      Examples of NOT varied values: hard work, determination, perseverance
      Examples of more varied values: autonomy, resourcefulness, healthy boundaries, diversity

2. Vulnerability
   → Does the essay sound like it's mostly analytical or like it's coming from a deeper, more vulnerable place? (Another way of asking this: Does it sound like the author wrote it using mostly his or her head [intellect] or his or her heart and gut?)
   → After reading the essay, do you know more about the author AND feel closer to him or her?

3. "So what" moments (a.k.a. important and interesting connections)
   → Can you identify at least three to five "so what" moments of insight in the essay?
   → Are these moments predictable, or are they truly illuminating?

4. Craft
   → Do the ideas in the essay connect in a way that is logical, but not too obvious (boring)?

→ Can you tell that the essay represents a series of carefully considered choices and that the author spent a lot of time revising the essay over the course of several drafts?

→ Is it interesting and succinct throughout? If not, where do you lose interest? Where could words be cut or which part isn't revealing as much as it could be?

If you're feeling bold...

Give your essay to someone else and ask him or her to evaluate it based on these elements. But before you do, read "How and When to Ask for Feedback" on page 204.

Want to read some example essays that incorporate all these elements?

Guess what: I've already given you a bunch of examples, since most of the essays in this book illustrate these qualities.

To clarify these qualities, you'll find four of my favorite essays in chapter nine, and in the analysis that follows each one, I've highlighted the qualities discussed in The Great College Essay Test (see page 186).

If you don't want to read examples right now, though, and you just want to know how to improve your own essay based on these criteria, keep reading.

HOW TO BRING MORE VALUES, VULNERABILITY, AND INSIGHT INTO YOUR ESSAY (OR HOW TO IMPROVE YOUR ESSAY IF YOU FEEL IT'S "JUST OKAY")

In this section I address:

1. How to Bring More Values (and Information!) into Your Essay
2. How to Be Vulnerable in Your Essay
3. How to Make Sure Your Insights Are Actually Insightful

If you've skipped to this section and you're not yet sure if your essay is great or just okay, flip back to page 186 and give your essay The Great College Essay Test.

1. How to Bring More Values (and Information!) into Your Essay

Just a reminder that when I say it's important to include "information" in your essay, I don't mean trivial facts; I mean core values (see the Core Values Exercise on page 8 for examples).

I believe it's important to clearly express four to five of your core values in the essay. Here's how:

Make sure you've done the Core Values Exercise on page 8. And, if you know what career you're aiming for, make sure you've identified the values necessary for that career (see page 59 in the "How to Write Essay Type B" section for more on how to do this).

Then ask yourself these three questions:

1. Which values are clearly coming through in the essay? Highlight the lines that clearly demonstrate those values.
2. Which values are kind of coming through but could be expressed more clearly?
3. Which values aren't there yet, but could be?

> Tip: Delete any repetitive values. Examples: "determination" and "perseverance" are basically the same thing, as are "collaboration" and "working with others." But if you feel they are definitely different, just make sure to articulate why they're different.

In short, make sure you're exhibiting a variety of values. Then:

CUT sections where no values are clearly being communicated, REWRITE sections where the values aren't super clear, and ADD sections that will clearly communicate values that aren't there yet, but that you'd like to include.

2. How to Be Vulnerable in Your Essay

I'm sometimes asked: Must you be vulnerable to write a great essay? The answer is no. I've read some great essays that are not, in some way, vulnerable. (Pause.) Okay, actually, I just went through this book looking for examples of great essays that aren't in some way vulnerable, and I couldn't find one. So the answer might be yes.

Why? Because there are so many ways to be vulnerable in your essay. Here are a few of those ways:

Reveal Something That You Worry People Might Judge You For

This is a common way to define vulnerability: we fear revealing something that might lead us to feel isolated, ashamed, or unloved. But I find that vulnerability can, in fact, have the opposite effect. By discussing our deepest fears, we can actually draw people closer to us, since deep down we often share those same fears.

Here are some essays by students who were worried that they might be judged for their essay content: "Raising Anthony," "Easter," "Bowling," "What I Found on the Farm," "I Shot My Brother," "Breaking Up with Mom," and especially "Knife."

I want to emphasize that, by the end of each of the essays listed, I don't feel repelled by the authors—quite the opposite, actually. I want to know them better because the choice to be vulnerable is a brave and risky choice, and I like brave people who take risks.

The other benefit is a little more mysterious—the vulnerable place is, I believe, where the magic happens. Venture down the path of vulnerability and who knows where it might lead, but chances are it will be somewhere interesting.

Discuss a Challenge or Contradiction That Is Unresolved or Unresolvable

One thing I don't find very interesting in a personal statement is a student presenting his or her résumé or activities list. Here's why: Admissions officers are less interested in who you have been, and they're more interested in who you are becoming. I sometimes describe this difference as writing to report vs. writing to discover. Writing to report says, "I'm finished and here is what I'm presenting," whereas writing to discover says, "I'm very much in process and this is what I've figured out so far, but here are one or two things I haven't figured out yet." In essence, while answers are okay, good questions are more interesting.

So where can you search for your own unresolved challenges or contradictions? Often these are the result of a conflict between important values. What do I mean?

Here are some personal examples of my own unresolved challenges and the values that I believe are in conflict:

- I want to eat foods that are good for me (value: health), but this is at odds with my desire to eat every different kind of pizza on the planet (values: freedom, curiosity, variety, authenticity).
- I want to be present with my daughter (values: family, connection), but I also really love traveling to deliver workshops for students, parents, and counselors (values: meaningful work, variety, connection).

See what I mean? And note that this concept of conflicting values is actually the essence of drama. Think about that: drama doesn't exist if you hate X but love Y. Drama exists when you love two things that are in opposition. (There's no drama if I love eating healthy foods and hate eating pizza, since the choice is simple: don't eat pizza. Drama exists when I crave eating a whole pizza, but I also want to lead a healthy, balanced lifestyle.)

In terms of your essay, these types of conflict can create what I call a productive tension, one that may be worth exploring in an essay.

How can you discover these for yourself?

Review your top values from the Core Values Exercise on page 8 and ask: Which of my other top values tends to conflict with this one? (Here's an example, with values marked in bold: my desire for **consistency** sometimes conflicts with my desire to **travel**, or my desire to **express myself** often conflicts with my desire to **listen**.) And here's the key: try to find something that you haven't figured out yet (in other words, an unresolved conflict), and then go write about it. See what happens. Or if you've written a draft already that you feel isn't all that deep, use the Feelings and Needs Exercise on page 127 and see if you can determine which needs are in conflict. Note that sometimes we encounter conflicts that aren't just unresolved, but are actually unresolvable. And that can be even more interesting.

For example, sometimes I will listen to meditation CDs while I'm driving in order to be productive and efficient. But think about that. This represents two directly opposed values—my desire to do more (multitask) and my desire to just be (meditate). What does this say about me? It's a complex question. When should I do, and when should I just be? It's the dance of life, and I don't know that I can actually resolve it. But that's okay. I believe facing down our unresolved or unresolvable conflicts and contradictions reveals us as vulnerable, as human.

For an example of an essay that addresses an unresolvable contradiction or paradox, check out the "Barbie vs. Terrorism and the Patriarchy" essay on page 207.

Describe Your Passion and Do Not Apologize for It

How does this show vulnerability? Because it takes guts to stand up and say what you love, or what you stand for, especially if your passion is something other people might consider nerdy, like reading or, God forbid, endodontics. (I say this with love: I am a nerd too—for college essays, board games, and puns.) But it's possible to scream to the heavens "I LOVE MATH" unapologetically, and people will love you for it.

But here's the key: you can't just say, "I love math so, so, so much." You still need to make sure that your essay reveals core values, includes "so what" moments of insight, and is well-crafted.

Three essays that I find to be unapologetically passionate are the "Endodontics," "If Ink Were Ants," and "Mazes" essays.

But want to get next-level vulnerable?

Discuss a Challenge and Don't Actually Resolve It at the End

Like this student did:

"BREAKING UP WITH MOM"

I stare into my cappuccino to try to avoid looking at my teary eyed mom, who had just found a hole in her favorite bright pink floral print scarf.

"I'm your mother, Katyush," she says in her heavy Russian accent.

A tiny bird of a woman with clipped wings.

I remember white walls, bottles upon bottles of acrylic paint, and a mortgage on a two-bedroom apartment in Lomita, California: my mother's dream. Together, we unpacked the painting box and started a mural on my new bedroom wall. "Let it Be", my new wall read, with an array of squares and swirls in every shade of blue imaginable. We proudly took a step back, then unpacked the Jasmine Fancy tea leaves and floral teapot.

Her trembling hands reach for her coffee.

"You're supposed to take care of me. That's what family does. I don't have anyone else."

Her mom in Moscow, her ex-husband remarried, and her oldest son avoiding her at all costs. Unemployed and unwilling.

"I'll get my pills eventually, but family has responsibilities."

Her depression plummeting, her sanity dwindling, her only lifeline dying for freedom from her confines.

I flash back to the terror in her eyes as she noticed a chip on the teapot's spout—a spark of fear that transformed into a thunderstorm. How she crumpled in the old kitchen chair across from me. From that moment on, life became a broken record. I walked her to bed, kissed her goodnight, reminded her that I had school the next day. Asleep by 3 am. Late to class. Come home stressed. Start homework. Take care of mom. Finish homework. 3 am.

My mother was in a state of stagnation, and she had a hold on me like quicksand.

Though living with my dad and stepmom was its own ticking timebomb, for the most part I was left alone long enough to do schoolwork and get to class on time—but every moment away from my mom felt like I was tying a noose around her neck. Nothing I did could bring her the peace she wanted from me.

When I was fifteen years old I broke up with my mother. We could still be friends, I told her, but I needed my space, and she couldn't give me that.

For the first time in my life, I had taken action. I was never again going to passively let life happen to me.

During four long months of separation, I filled the space that my mom previously dominated with learning: everything and anything. I began teaching myself rudimentary French through an online program, learned basic HTML coding and website design, and began editing my drawings on Photoshop so that I could sell them online. When my dad lost his job, I learned to sew my own clothing, and applied my new knowledge to costume design within the Drama department.

On stage, I learned to stand up and say things that mattered. Backstage, I worked with teams of dedicated students who wanted each other to succeed. In our improv group, I gained the confidence to act on my instincts. In the classroom, my Drama teacher emulated the person I wanted to be. She gave me hugs on days that wouldn't end, insisted that taking care of myself was not the same thing as being selfish, and most importantly, taught me how to ask for help.

A year later, it all culminated in One Bad Apple—a full length musical that I produced with my best friend. Managing the budget, scheduling rehearsals, and working with a cast and crew of students was easily the most difficult thing I have ever done—but it was my choice. The challenge, and the reward, belonged to me.

On my sixteenth birthday, I picked up the phone and dialed my mom. I waited through three agonizingly long pauses between rings.

"Katyush?"

"Hi mom, it's me."

I absolutely love this essay. Why? Because the author doesn't follow the standard "...but I learned from and was shaped by this experience," a common trope for failure essays. *Yet I still learn a lot about this student's core values, plus it's loaded with "so what" moments.* And in terms of craft, this is next-level stuff; it's clear that the words were carefully chosen and that the author revised over several drafts.

What can we learn from this?

1. You don't need to tie things up at the end with a nice little bow. Your essay can finish in an open-ended way.
2. If you decide not to tie things up at the end, the rest of the essay had better be amazing. And how do you know if your essay is amazing? Write ten drafts until you find it to be amazing, then give it to five people and ask them if they agree.
3. There are many ways to be vulnerable, and this essay employs all the methods I've described so far. The author:

a. reveals something people might judge her for (her tumultuous relationship with her family, in particular her mom),

b. addresses an unresolved challenge (inner conflict between her desire to help her mom, which has led her to frustration, and her desire to be free and focus on her own needs—put simply, the conflicting values might be "helping others" vs. "helping herself"), and

c. names a passion for which she does not apologize (it could be argued that this is theater—and if you met this student you'd know this is her passion—but I think there's a deeper passion unfolding here, since by the end of the essay she is learning to fall in love with herself).

> Tip: One variation on the method just described is to discuss a failure you experienced and to not (as most students do) actually resolve everything at the end. One student I worked with, for example, discussed how a student he was tutoring in an after-school program ended up quitting the program. Rather than making things nice in the conclusion of his essay, though, he reflected on how he felt he had failed that student and in the end is left with the burden of that failure. It was powerful.

So ask yourself: What would the Hollywood ending to my essay be? Then reject that Hollywood ending and ask yourself: What really happened? And what's the deeper lesson I can learn based on that?

How to Practice Being Vulnerable: Complete the Feelings and Needs Exercise on Page 127 with Someone You Know

Here's an idea: complete the Feelings and Needs Exercise on page 127 by picking something that really bothers you about someone you know (maybe you feel that a friend doesn't really listen to you, for example, or that your coach doesn't treat you as being equal to the others on your team). Then tell the person how you feel about that and what your deeper needs are. This may or may not give you

content for your essay, but it should give you a pretty good reference point for what vulnerability feels like! Also, imagining that
conversation may have made your stomach drop just now. If so,
that may be an indication you're on the right path to vulnerability.

3. How to Make Sure Your Insights Are Actually Insightful

Consider that providing insight is like telling a joke, and that joke
telling is basic setup and payoff. A funny joke positions the setup and
payoff just the right mental distance apart. If the setup and payoff are
too close to each other, the joke isn't that funny:

Q: Why did the chicken cross the road?
A: To get to the other side.

But if the setup and payoff are too far apart, the joke isn't funny either:

Q: What's the difference between a watermelon and a sweet pea?
A: About ten minutes.

(This is an old family joke that relies on telling the joke aloud.
Good luck. It took me years to get it.)

For an insight to be satisfying, your setup has to be just the right
mental distance from your payoff. Here's what I mean by "mental
distance" and how to do this:

Separate several of your "show" moments from your "tell" moments.

To clarify, a "show" moment is an interesting image, detail, example,
or story that illustrates a core value or an important point, and a "tell"
moment offers some comment on or interpretation of that "show."

Example "show" moment:

> Many nights you'll find me in the garage replacing standard chrome trim with an elegant piano black finish or changing the threads on the stitching of the seats to add a personal touch...

Example "tell" moment:

> ...as I believe a few small changes can transform a generic product into a personalized work of art.

Note: I think these are the right "mental distance" from each other because I wouldn't be likely to guess the "tell" simply by reading the "show."

Okay, once you've separated your "show" and "tell" moments:

a. Read your "show" moments aloud to someone else and see if he or she can predict what your insight will be.

b. If that person can predict your insight, chances are your current insight isn't surprising or unusual. So rewrite the insight. And if you can't come up with something insightful, consider cutting the image/detail/example/story altogether.

What about Craft?

You'll notice that I included four qualities in The Great College Essay Test, but I only discuss how to do the first three here. Why? Because, in some sense, this whole book is about craft—and to try to say in a few paragraphs, "Here's how to craft your essay" would be just plain silly. So if you're looking for my answer to how to write a well-crafted college essay, my answer is this book. All of it.

But there is a little something called "style" that I'd love to offer a few tips on, and it's not unrelated to craft. So here are:

A Few Ways to Score Style Points (Once Your Essay Is Mostly Written)

1. Express complex thoughts in succinct ways
This simply means taking something elaborate and saying it in fewer words.

Examples:

In the "Breaking Up with Mom" essay (page 192), the author details a complicated relationship with her mother. But rather than going into all the details of how complicated her mother is, she evokes it in these two lines:

> "I'm your mother, Katyush," she says in her heavy Russian accent.
> A tiny bird of a woman with clipped wings.

And just like that we learn a whole lot. Does she spell it out? No. But we do learn something valuable about the way the author sees her mother.

Here's another example, from the "Grandma's Kimchi" essay (page 209):

> A piece of writing is more than just a piece of writing. It evokes.
> It inspires. It captures what time takes away.
>   My grandma used to say: "Tigers leave furs when they die, humans leave their names." Her legacy was the smell of garlic that lingered around my house. Mine will be these words.

Again, the author communicates so much in just a few words. And in this essay, those last five words deliver that satisfying "surprising, but inevitable" conclusion that I'm such a fan of (see page 150 for more).

How to express a complex thought in a succinct way:
First, you'll need a complex thought. To get one, you'll need to think deeply about your world, and you'll need to question your own assumptions.

Can't think of a complex thought? You're in trouble. Give up writing an essay altogether.

I'm kidding.

Instead, try looking through your essay and, for each major point you make, ask yourself these four questions:

1. What are the positive/negative consequences of this belief?
2. What's a potential counterargument for this belief that I can debunk?
3. What's a call to action? (What must I do as a result?)
4. What's an unexpected value? (Is there something else that I or we will gain if we learn from or put this belief into action?)

In essence, you're answering "So what?" These four questions are designed to help you do that. Your goal is to come up with a fresh idea.

Next, you'll need to find a succinct way to explain your fresh idea. How? By revising, revising, and revising some more. If you've written something, revised it, and it's still unclear, chances are it's because your thoughts aren't clear—yet. Keep going. Keep whittling away the unnecessary. You'll get there.

2. Use big words selectively

First, some examples:

From the "With Debate" essay (page 22): "My diffidence was frustrating" and "as calls for help grew, the more defunct I became." Note the simple but effective use of the words "diffidence" and "defunct." Their use isn't showy, the words are used correctly, and there are only two big words—not six.

From the "Knife" essay (page 144): "I was at my most desperate. My friend had died in September of my junior year. Five AP classes, weekly volunteering, and a tutoring job had provided added stress. I needed reprieve. And I found it in the knife." Note the use of the word "reprieve." Again, simple.

From the "Mazes" essay (page 211): "...I created several computer

games, incorporating such unordinary aspects of gameplay as the avoidance of time-travel paradoxes, and the control of 'jounce,' the fourth
derivative of position with respect to time." Okay, so this example is a
little less selective in terms of its usage of big words, and you'll need to
decide for yourself how far you want to go with this, but I wanted to
show you an example that was a little more showy. But I wouldn't go
too much further than this example with your jargon/geeky language
(see page 114 for more on using geeky language).

What not to do:

Don't add needless complexity. "Obscurantism is obscurantism,"
as my English teacher Mrs. Clark used to say.

What do I mean? Don't do this:

> I have experienced the unbridgeable paradigm between a
> dissipated way of life and a miring in depression and lack
> of motivation. The moment I apprehended the myriad of
> consistencies between the diversified fields of religion,
> philosophy, and existence, I eliminated the sufferings caused
> by my inextricable subjectivity, and eventually surrendered
> to the conclusion—after analyzing the mechanism of the
> universe and the history of evolution—that everything is
> without clear meaning.

In short, when it comes to big words, be like my man Prufrock:
politic, cautious, and meticulous.

3. Make the reader cry

This one's kind of a joke because I mean, really, how do you *make*
the reader cry?

Well, I'll tell you.

1. Tap into something so deep and important to you that just
   thinking about it makes you cry. Then:

2. Write about it in a way that never, ever, makes the reader feel like you're trying to make him or her cry.
3. Finally, make sure to leave something unaccounted for. (The best essays don't explain everything.)

Examples of essays that have made me cry: the "Bowling," "Dying Bird," "I Shot My Brother," "Grandma's Kimchi," and "Breaking Up with Mom" essays.

How do you test this? Keep revising it until your essay makes five different people cry.

But remember: Do it without trying to do it.

WHEN TO SCRAP WHAT YOU HAVE AND START OVER

When is it time to start over? Simple:

Any time you want.

As long as it's before the deadline, you have time.

Really?

In the words of Shrek, "Really, really." As writers, we can sometimes grow pretty attached to what we've written. We think, "But I've spent so much time on it!" or "I'm invested!" or my favorite, "If I start over now, I'll *lose* everything I've written!"

But it's not true. You won't *lose* anything. Just because you choose new examples, a new structure, or even a new topic doesn't mean you lose everything from before. The work you've done clears the way for the work you've yet to do.

"Sacrifice the essay of yesterday to the essay of tomorrow."

—ME (I THINK)

If you're feeling kind of "meh" about your essay, or like you haven't found your deepest story yet, just remember:
There's an extraordinary story inside you waiting to be told.

"Ditch your crappy story so your extraordinary story can come forth."

—ALBERT EINSTEIN (I'M KIDDING. THAT'S ME, TOO.)

HOW TO WRITE YOUR ESSAY IN JUST ONE NIGHT (BREAK ONLY IN CASE OF EMERGENCY)

Please. Try *everything* else before you try this. Why? Because writing a great personal statement takes time. How much time? In my experience, a great essay takes several weeks to write, and most of the essays in this book represent the fifth, sixth, or fifteenth draft.

But what if you don't have the luxury of time? Say you're in a jam and, for whatever reason, your essay is due in a few days (or hours). That's what this section is for.

Here's what to do:

Create an outline based on qualities or values you'd like to show, but instead of ending the essay with your future career, end with values that will be important to you no matter what career you choose.

Here's how to do it:

1. Complete the first five items on the "Six Ways to Generate Your Content" list on page 91.
2. Get a blank sheet of paper, draw a vertical line down the middle, write the words "My values" at the top of the right column, and list your four to five most important values with space in between. (Example: "knowledge"—skip an inch—"nature"—skip an inch—"music.") That's right, you're doing a modified type B essay.
3. In the left column, beside each value, describe an image that shows how you developed that value. (Examples: Beside the value of "knowledge" you write, "I sometimes stay up until 3 a.m. surfing obscure Wikipedia articles," or beside the value of "nature" you write, "Going camping alone with just a tent, my journal, and 5 lbs. of trail mix.") You get the idea. Everything in the left column should be visual, like a snapshot or a scene from a movie.
4. Put your little movies in order—chronological often works—and describe each image or movie in a brief paragraph. (Important: Don't mention your values yet.)
5. Write transitions between the ideas so there is some sense of flow. This part will take the longest. (Hint: If you write them chronologically, you can use basic transitions such as "A few years later…" or "When I entered high school…" as place-holders and tweak later.)
6. At the end, describe some of the values that you'll carry with you into college and beyond.

This will at least yield an essay that demonstrates a few of your core values. With any extra time you have, try including a "so what" moment after each value. For more on this, turn to page 62.

For examples of what this might look like, check out the "Scrapbook" (page 28) and "Punk Rock Philosopher" (page 96) essays, both of which use a simple framing device to lay out some important details and then end with some core values. I'm not saying, by the way, that these essays were written in one night, but they were written more quickly than some of the other essays in this book.

HOW AND WHEN TO ASK FOR FEEDBACK

Getting opinions from others is a great idea—when it's done the right way. Here are some common mistakes to avoid and some tips for what to do instead.

1. Don't ask for feedback too early.

When an idea is newly hatched, it's very fragile. A harsh word can stop it dead.

> Tip: Wait 'til you're really, really ready.

2. Don't ask for feedback from too many people.

"Too many cooks spoil the broth," goes the old saying. It's so true.

> Tip: During the writing process, I recommend working with one person at a time. Once you're clear on what every single paragraph is doing and why every single sentence and word is there, then it's safe to ask a few more people. But wait until you feel really solid about what you've produced.

3. Don't be vague (or lie to yourself) about what kind of feedback you want.

> Tip: If you know or sense that you're looking for something specific, do your reader (and yourself) a favor and ask for that specific thing. (Example

email: "Hi, Mrs. Clark! I've written a draft of my college essay and I'm wondering if you would mind proofreading it. I'm happy with the topic and the structure, so I don't need feedback on that; I just want to make sure I don't have any glaring grammatical errors. Thanks!") It's such a big help to your teachers/counselors/friends/family-members-turned-editors.

Sometimes you honestly just want to hear, "Great essay! Submit it!" Or say it's twenty-four hours from a submission deadline. Who wants to be told, "I think you should write about your involvement with wrestling instead." Yikes. Nobody. The more specific you are with your feedback request, the more likely you are to get what you want from the exchange.

Something to keep in mind: consider that essays work in three parts—content (what the essay is about), structure (how the ideas connect to one another), and details—and it's sometimes hard to give notes on one without giving notes on the other. If you ask for someone to give notes on the "structure" or "flow" of the essay, that can be difficult because sometimes an essay isn't working because of the topic, not because of the structure. So don't be afraid to ask your reader for feedback on the topic and structure—just be ready to hear that person say, "I'm not sure this is the best topic for you," since that may mean that the reader is suggesting you start over. Must you start over? No (see next point). But you might want to consider it (see earlier section "When to Scrap What You Have and Start Over" on page 201).

4. Don't allow one person's opinion to be more important than your own.

Who knows, objectively, what every single college admissions reader will think? No one. And anyone who claims to know "what colleges want" is often really saying, "Here is what I've seen work for some other students."

Tip: If you hear someone giving general writing advice, request specificity. (Example: If your counselor, or even a college admissions person, says something like, "The essay should be in your authentic voice," feel free to ask, "What does 'authentic voice' mean to you?" or "How do I do that?".) If you agree with what the person says and it's useful, great! If it's vague or doesn't resonate with you, then see my note below.

A Quick Final Note on How to Receive Feedback

Remember: Anyone's input is just that—input. It doesn't mean you have to follow it. If you're given advice on how to write your essay that you don't agree with—either from your parents, your friend, your counselor, or even from me—don't be afraid to ask, "Why?" And if the answer doesn't make sense, or you don't think it will help, just nod graciously and thank the person for the input. Deep down, that person likely has your best interests at heart and is just trying to help.

But it's your essay. It's your story. You get final say.

CHAPTER NINE

A Few of My Favorite Essays

I LOVE ALL THE ESSAYS in this book, but coming up are a few that I believe pass The Great College Essay Test, as they exhibit core values, vulnerability, "so what" moments, and craft. Read them first here, without comment, then read my analysis afterward.

"BARBIE VS. TERRORISM AND THE PATRIARCHY"

Much of my early knowledge of how the world works was formed through countless hours spent playing with Barbie dolls. My sister, Taylor, and I had a plethora of toys, filling our basement's cabinets and often littering our brightly checkered IKEA rug, but Barbie was our favorite. We gave her choppy, unfortunate haircuts, houses constructed out of large wooden dominoes, and a variety of cars—a neon orange truck, a convertible with a bubblegum-pink steering wheel, and a Volkswagen Beetle with a missing back tire.

Above the basement, the kitchen radio spewed out information—the news of the 9/11 attacks on our friends' parents at the Pentagon, the War in Afghanistan, and the D.C. area snipers' attacks on our entire community—but Taylor and I had trouble understanding what the information meant.

As my mom drove me to a doctor's appointment, our local station announced that the snipers had shot someone just miles away. After I "raced" her inside into the waiting room, I soaked in the murmur about guns, a white van, and two very bad men. In the car ride home, I asked her a myriad of questions about terrorism including, "Do bullets go through glass?" Her responses left me still craving answers, so I took matters into my own hands. At five years old, I decided to enlist Barbie in the army.

While I fought against my penetrating fear of the world outside our haven of toys, Barbie herself fought against the very terrorism I was afraid of. In what we called our "Barbie Afghanistan," Taylor and I worked through our confusion by making Barbie fight the battles, still wearing her high heels and ball gowns.

I no longer play with Barbie, but she has fought another war in my adolescence. I'm a passionate feminist, and my opinions about Barbie have caused an internal tug-of-war on my beliefs. As I sit in my basement now, surrounded by books and my laptop, I have just as many questions as I did at five years old.

I've desperately attempted to consolidate my opposing opinions of Barbie into a single belief, but I've accepted that they're separate. In one, she has perpetuated physical ideals unrepresentative of how real female bodies are built. Striving to look like Barbie is not only striving for the impossible—the effort is detrimental to women's psychological and physical health, including my own. In the other, Barbie has inspired me in her breaking of the plastic ceiling. She has dabbled in close to 150 careers, including some I'd love to have: a UNICEF Ambassador, teacher, and business executive. And although it's not officially listed on her résumé, Barbie served honorably in the War in Afghanistan.

Barbie has proven to be an 11.5-inch-tall embodiment of both what frustrates and excites me. From terrorism to feminism and beyond, I am vexed by the complexities of the world but eager to piece things together. Although I'm frustrated by what I can't understand, I've realized that confusion is okay.

With Barbie as my weapon, I've continued to fight in the many "wars" in my life. I've found great value in the questions I ask and in my attempts to reconcile our world's inevitable contradictions. Things can be innocent yet mature, they can be detrimental yet empowering, and they can even wear high heels and a ball gown while fighting in a war.

"GRANDMA'S KIMCHI"

Every Saturday morning, I'd awaken to the smell of crushed garlic and piquant pepper. I would stumble into the kitchen to find my grandma squatting over a large silver bowl, mixing fat lips of fresh cabbages with garlic, salt, and red pepper. That was how the delectable Korean dish, kimchi, was born every weekend at my home.

My grandma's specialty always dominated the dinner table as kimchi filled every plate. And like my grandma who had always been living with us, it seemed as though the luscious smell of garlic would never leave our home. But even the prided recipe was defenseless against the ravages of Alzheimer's that inflicted my grandma's mind.

Dementia slowly fed on her memories until she became as blank as a brand-new notebook. The ritualistic rigor of Saturday mornings came to a pause, and during dinner, the artificial taste of vacuum-packaged factory kimchi only emphasized the absence of the family tradition. I would look at her and ask,

"Grandma, what's my name?" But she would stare back at me with a clueless expression. Within a year of diagnosis, she lived with us like a total stranger.

One day, my mom brought home fresh cabbages and red pepper sauce. She brought out the old silver bowl and poured out the cabbages, smothering them with garlic and salt and pepper. The familiar tangy smell tingled my nose. Gingerly, my grandma stood up from the couch in the living room, and as if lured by the smell, sat by the silver bowl and dug her hands into the spiced cabbages. As her bony hands shredded the green lips, a look of determination grew on her face. Though her withered hands no longer displayed the swiftness and precision they once did, her face showed the aged rigor of a professional. For the first time in years, the smell of garlic filled the air and the rattling of the silver bowl resonated throughout the house.

That night, we ate kimchi. It wasn't perfect; the cabbages were clumsily cut and the garlic was a little too strong. But kimchi had never tasted better. I still remember my grandma putting a piece in my mouth and saying, "Here, Dong Jin. Try it, my boy."

Seeing grandma again this summer, that moment of clarity seemed ephemeral. Her disheveled hair and expressionless face told of the aggressive development of her illness.

But holding her hands, looking into her eyes, I could still smell that garlic. The moments of Saturday mornings remain ingrained in my mind. Grandma was an artist who painted the cabbages with strokes of red pepper. Like the sweet taste of kimchi, I hope to capture those memories in my keystrokes as I type away these words.

A piece of writing is more than just a piece of writing. It evokes. It inspires. It captures what time takes away.

My grandma used to say: "Tigers leave furs when they die, humans leave their names." Her legacy was the smell of garlic that lingered around my house. Mine will be these words.

"MAZES"

My story begins at about the age of two, when I first learned what a maze was. For most people, solving mazes is a childish phase, but I enjoyed artistically designing them. Eventually my creations jumped from their two dimensional confinement, requiring the solver to dive through holes to the other side, or fold part of the paper over, then right back again. At around the age of eight, I invented a way for mazes to carry binary-encoded messages, with left turns and right turns representing 0s and 1s. This evolved into a base-3 maze on the surface of a tetrahedron, with crossing an edge representing a 2. For me, a blank piece of paper represented the freedom to explore new dimensions, pushing the boundaries of traditional maze making.

I found a similar freedom in mathematics. Here's what I wrote when I was 9:

$N + B = Z$

$M^2 = P$

$E - (L + B) = G$

$C / Y = Z - Q$

$B + B = Y$

$(D - V)^9 - (P*L) = J$

$W = (I - V)^2$

$Y + B + C = R$

$O^2 + (Y*O) = T$

$F^3 - (T + W) = F^2$

$V - R = H - U$

$A^3 - C = N$

$Y^2 + B = L$

$J^2 - J = J + (P + I)$

$Y^3 = X$

$X - R = M - O$

$D*A - B - (V + Y) = E$

$$U - X - O = W$$
$$P / P = B$$
$$S - A = U$$
$$(Z + B)*C = P$$
$$C(+ / -)B = A$$
$$U + C = H$$
$$R - L = S - T$$

The object of puzzles like these was to solve for every letter, assuming they each represented a unique positive integer, and that both sides of each equation are positive. These are not typical assumptions for practical mathematics, and I didn't even need 26 equations. Upon formally learning algebra, I was dismayed that "proper math" operated under a different set of assumptions, that two variables can be equal, or be non-integers, and that you always need as many equations as variables. Yet looking back, I now see that mathematics was so inspirational because there really is no "proper" way, no convention to hold me from discovering a completely original method of thought. Math was, and still is, yet another way for me to freely express my creativity and different way of thinking without constraint.

It's all about freedom. The thoughts are there, they just need a way to escape. The greatest single advancement that delivered even more freedom was my first computer, and on it, one of the first computer games I ever played: "Maze Madness." It was a silly and simple game, but I remember being awed that I could create my own levels. Through the years, I've made thousands (not exaggerating) of levels in a variety of different computer games. I get most excited when I discover a bug that I can incorporate to add a new twist to the traditional gameplay.

A few years ago I grew tired of working within the constraints of most internet games and I wanted to program my own, so I decided to learn the language of Scratch. With it, I created several computer games, incorporating such unordinary aspects of gameplay as the avoidance of time-travel paradoxes, and the control of "jounce," the fourth derivative of position with respect to time. Eventually, I came to realize that Scratch was too limited to implement some of my ideas, so I learned C#, and my potential expanded exponentially. I continue to study programming knowing that the more I learn, the more tools I have to express my creativity.

I plan to design computer systems that are as outside of the box as my thoughts. And who knows where it will lead? My way of thinking in different dimensions could be the very thing separating computers from humans, and it could motivate the creation of true artificial intelligence. To me, studying computer science is the next step of an evolution of boundary breaking that has been underway since my first maze.

ANALYSIS OF A FEW OF MY FAVORITE ESSAYS

As I've already analyzed a few essays based on narrative structure or montage structure (page 30) and the "Four Qualities of an Amazing Essay" (page 178), I'll analyze the following essays in terms of the qualities of The Great College Essay Test, which are:

1. Core values (information)
2. Vulnerability
3. "So what" moments (insights or important and interesting connections)
4. Craft

"BARBIE VS. TERRORISM AND
THE PATRIARCHY"

Much of my early knowledge of how the world works was formed through countless hours spent playing with Barbie dolls. My sister, Taylor, and I had a plethora of toys, filling our basement's cabinets and often littering our brightly checkered IKEA rug, but Barbie was our favorite. We gave her choppy, unfortunate haircuts, houses constructed out of large wooden dominoes, and a variety of cars—a neon orange truck, a convertible with a bubblegum-pink steering wheel, and a Volkswagen Beetle with a missing back tire.

Craft. Love the details/ verisimilitude here. And not too much, just enough.

Above the basement, the kitchen radio spewed out information—the news of the 9/11 attacks on our friends' parents at the Pentagon, the War in Afghanistan, and the D.C. area snipers' attacks on our entire community—but Taylor and I had trouble understanding what the information meant.

As my mom drove me to a doctor's appointment, our local station announced that the snipers had shot someone just miles away. After I "raced" her inside into the waiting room, I soaked in the murmur about guns, a white van, and two very bad men. In the car ride home, I asked her a myriad of questions about terrorism including, "Do bullets go through glass?" Her responses left me still craving answers, so I took matters into my own hands. At five years old, I decided to enlist Barbie in the army.

Information. Core value: curiosity.

While I fought against my penetrating fear of the world outside our haven of toys, Barbie herself fought against the very terrorism I was afraid of. In what we called our "Barbie Afghanistan," Taylor and I worked through our confusion by making Barbie fight the battles, still wearing her high heels and ball gowns.

Information. Core values: creativity and social consciousness (even at a young age).

I no longer play with Barbie, but she has fought another war in my adolescence. I'm a passionate feminist, and my opinions about Barbie have caused an internal tug-of-war on my beliefs. As I sit in my basement now, surrounded by books and my laptop, I have just as many questions as I did at five years old. I've desperately attempted to consolidate my opposing opinions of Barbie into a single belief, but I've accepted that they're separate. In one, she has perpetuated physical ideals unrepresentative of how real female bodies are built. Striving to look like Barbie is not only striving for the impossible—the effort is detrimental to women's psychological and physical health, including my own. In the other, Barbie has inspired me in her breaking of the plastic ceiling. She has dabbled in close to 150 careers, including some I'd love to have: a UNICEF Ambassador, teacher, and business executive. And although it's not officially listed on her résumé, Barbie served honorably in the War in Afghanistan.

Barbie has proven to be an 11.5-inch-tall embodiment of both what frustrates and excites me. From terrorism to feminism and beyond, I am vexed by the complexities of the world but eager to piece things together. Although I'm frustrated by what I can't understand, I've realized that confusion is okay.

With Barbie as my weapon, I've continued to fight in the many "wars" in my life. I've found great value in the questions I ask and in my attempts to reconcile our world's inevitable contradictions. Things can be innocent yet mature, they can be detrimental yet empowering, and they can even wear high heels and a ball gown while fighting in a war.

Important and interesting connection (a.k.a. "so what" moment).

In a society that sometimes insists students have their lives mapped out, this can be a scary thing to admit. Important and interesting connections. GREAT "so what." Vulnerability!

Information, important and interesting connections, craft, vulnerability (and humor). Amazing paragraph—this one hits all the marks.

Great "so what," and the turn of phrase she uses at the end is beautifully crafted.

I learn so much about this student and her values. I learn that she is curious, funny, intelligent, socially aware, mature, and willing to be vulnerable. Plus, she's able to include some memorable turns of phrase and express complex thoughts in succinct ways. All without having to shoot her brother or watch a bird die.

"GRANDMA'S KIMCHI"

Note how this essay does NOT begin with a hook in the traditional sense of "grabbing the reader's attention." Instead, it begins quietly, with a dash of verisimilitude.

Every Saturday morning, I'd awaken to the smell of crushed garlic and piquant pepper. I would stumble into the kitchen to find my grandma squatting over a large silver bowl, mixing fat lips of fresh cabbages with garlic, salt, and red pepper. That was how the delectable Korean dish, kimchi, was born every weekend at my home.

Information and craft. Values of family, ritual, tradition, and community are established here in just a few words.

My grandma's specialty always dominated the dinner table as kimchi filled every plate. And like my grandma who had always been living with us, it seemed as though the luscious smell of garlic would never leave our home. But even the prided recipe was defenseless against the ravages of Alzheimer's that inflicted my grandma's mind.

Craft. Note the subtle double meaning of "fed."

Dementia slowly fed on her memories until she became as blank as a brand-new notebook. The ritualistic rigor of Saturday mornings came to a pause, and during dinner, the artificial taste of vacuum-packaged factory kimchi only emphasized the absence of the family tradition. I would look at her and ask, "Grandma, what's my name?" But she would stare back at me with a clueless expression. Within a year of diagnosis, she lived with us like a total stranger.

More craft. This is even more subtle, but it's foreshadowing the ending.

One day, my mom brought home fresh cabbages and red pepper sauce. She brought out the old silver bowl and poured out the cabbages, smothering them with garlic and salt and pepper. The familiar tangy smell tingled my nose. Gingerly, my grandma stood up from the couch in the living room, and as if lured by the smell, sat by the silver bowl and dug her hands into the spiced cabbages. As her bony hands shredded the green lips, a look of determination grew on her face. Though her withered hands no longer displayed the swiftness and precision they once did, her face showed the aged rigor of a professional. For the first time in years, the smell of garlic filled the air and the rattling of the silver bowl resonated throughout the house.

That night, we ate kimchi. It wasn't perfect; the cabbages were clumsily cut and the garlic was a little too strong. But kimchi had never tasted better. I still remember my grandma putting a piece in my mouth and saying, "Here, Dong Jin. Try it, my boy."

Holy craft, Batman. (I don't know about you, but I'm in tears.)

Seeing grandma again this summer, that moment of clarity seemed ephemeral. Her disheveled hair and expressionless face told of the aggressive development of her illness.

More craft. This is a student with some writing experience.

But holding her hands, looking into her eyes, I could still smell that garlic. The moments of Saturday mornings remain ingrained in my mind. Grandma was an artist who painted the cabbages with strokes of red pepper. Like the sweet taste of kimchi, I hope to capture those memories in my keystrokes as I type away these words.

BOOM. Super "so what" moment. And it's hugely vulnerable, too.

A piece of writing is more than just a piece of writing. It evokes. It inspires. It captures what time takes away.

I've been tempted to frame this and put it above my writing table. And I don't even need to say it, but CRAFT.

My grandma used to say: "Tigers leave furs when they die, humans leave their names." Her legacy was the smell of garlic that lingered around my house. Mine will be these words.

This is one of the very few effective uses of a quotation that I've ever seen. And it makes this ending so succinct, so memorable, and so…wow. Amazing use of craft, great "so what" moment, plus this clarifies some important values.

Again, I learn so much about this student through this essay. I learn that he values family, tradition, relationships, legacy, and the written word. This is one of the most well-crafted college essays I've read, and it makes me cry almost every time I read it.

"MAZES"

My story begins at about the age of two, when I first learned what a maze was. For most people, solving mazes is a childish phase, but I enjoyed artistically designing them. Eventually my creations jumped from their two dimensional confinement, requiring the solver to dive through holes to the other side, or fold part of the paper over, then right back again. At around the age of eight, I invented a way for mazes to carry binary-encoded messages, with left turns and right turns representing 0s and 1s. This evolved into a base-3 maze on the surface of a tetrahedron, with crossing an edge representing a 2.

For me, a blank piece of paper represented the freedom to explore new dimensions, pushing the boundaries of traditional maze making.

I found a similar freedom in mathematics. Here's what I wrote when I was 9:

$$N + B = Z$$
$$M^2 = P$$
$$E - (L + B) = G$$
$$C / Y = Z - Q$$
$$B + B = Y$$
$$(D - V)^9 - (P*L) = J$$
$$W = (I - V)^2$$
$$Y + B + C = R$$
$$O^2 + (Y*O) = T$$
$$F^3 - (T + W) = F^2$$
$$V - R = H - U$$
$$A^3 - C = N$$
$$Y^2 + B = L$$
$$J^2 - J = J + (P + I)$$
$$Y^3 = X$$
$$X - R = M - O$$

$$D*A - B - (V + Y) = E$$
$$U - X - O = W$$
$$P / P = B$$
$$S - A = U$$
$$(Z + B)*C = P$$
$$C(+/-)B = A$$
$$U + C = H$$
$$R - L = S - T$$

Values: creativity and risk. (How many students would have the guts to do this in an essay?)

The object of puzzles like these was to solve for every letter, assuming they each represented a unique positive integer, and that both sides of each equation are positive. These are not typical assumptions for practical mathematics, and I didn't even need 26 equations. Upon formally learning algebra, I was dismayed that "proper math" operated under a different set of assumptions, that two variables can be equal, or be non-integers, and that you always need as many equations as variables. Yet looking back, I now see that mathematics was so inspirational because there really is no "proper" way, no convention to hold me from discovering a completely original method of thought. Math was, and still is, yet another way for me to freely express my creativity and different way of thinking without constraint.

"So what" moment.

"So what" moment.

Craft. While he's expressing an important value (breaking convention), the content matches the form, since his equations break the convention of the standard college essay.

Value: freedom. In this case, he uses the value as a transition between his paragraphs.

It's all about freedom. The thoughts are there, they just need a way to escape. The greatest single advancement that delivered even more freedom was my first computer, and on it, one of the first computer games I ever played: "Maze Madness." It was a silly and simple game, but I remember being awed that I could create my own levels. Through the years, I've made thousands (not exaggerating) of levels in a variety of different computer games. I get most excited when I discover a bug that I can incorporate to add a new twist to the traditional gameplay.

Values: personal development, challenge, self-expression.

A few years ago I grew tired of working within the constraints of most internet games and I wanted to program my own, so I decided to learn the language of Scratch. With it, I

Values: personal development, challenge, self-expression.

created several computer games, incorporating such unordinary aspects of gameplay as the avoidance of time-travel paradoxes, and the control of "jounce," the fourth derivative of position with respect to time. Eventually, I came to realize that Scratch was too limited to implement some of my ideas, so I learned C#, and my potential expanded exponentially. I continue to study programming knowing that the more I learn, the more tools I have to express my creativity.

I plan to design computer systems that are as outside of the box as my thoughts. And who knows where it will lead? My way of thinking in different dimensions could be the very thing separating computers from humans, and it could motivate the creation of true artificial intelligence. To me, studying computer science is the next step of an evolution of boundary breaking that has been underway since my first maze.

"So what" moment.

Vulnerability. I believe he shows this through his passion. Why? It takes guts to say "I love math" in such a—and I say this with love—geeky way. He does it beautifully.

I love how this student's brain works. I love how much more he knows about math than I do, and I love how he makes math fun, creative, and inspiring—just like he is! I can feel his passion through his words, and this essay makes me curious to know more about him and the other amazing things he will create.

CHAPTER TEN

Finally

I'VE BEEN WORKING ON THIS book for a while. But my ideas keep evolving, and I feel I still haven't gotten it quite right. Here I sit, going over the manuscript five days before it's due to my editor, and I've got this T. S. Eliot line in my head: "That is not what I meant at all. That is not it, at all."

I stare at the blinking cursor, and I'm tempted to hit "delete" even on the end of the previous sentence, and to try saying it again, to say it better. Beckett is in my head now: "Try again. Fail again. Fail better."

But at some point, I know I've got to abandon the thing and send it out into the world.

Actually, I think that's the last thing I want to say to you.

I had a much longer speech prepared. But that thing that I just wrote is more important than what I had prepared.

Sometimes, writing is like this.

You work really hard to say a thing in just the right way, and then, after a little while, it's time to abandon it and send it out into the world.

So work really, really hard, my friend,

then let go.

Additional Resources

1,000+ WAYS TO GET INSPIRED RIGHT NOW

1. collegeessayguy.tumblr.com

   My Tumblr site is specifically dedicated to inspiring you as you work through the college essay process. It's updated almost daily, so you'll get up-to-date content that's specific to the time of year (i.e., essay tips in the fall, interview and financial aid tips in the winter, and so on).

2. collegeessayguy.com

   Here you'll find my most up-to-date resources for other parts of the application process, including:

   - How to Create a Great College List
   - How to Write a "Why Us" Essay
   - Five FAFSA Myths—Busted
   - College Interviews: How Much Do They Really Matter?
   - Five Common Myths about College Majors
   - Five Ways to Make Your Activities List Awesome
   - How to Decide Which Extracurricular Activity to Write About
   - How Much Do SAT Scores Matter? (A Paradox)

- How to Create the Simplest, Best To-Do List Ever
- 5 Resources That Will Save You $3,480

3. Google "100 Brave and Interesting Questions"
   This list is guaranteed to get your brain (and heart) going.

HOW TO WORK WITH A PARTNER

Why work with a partner?

1. He or she can hold you accountable.
2. He or she can serve as a mirror, reflecting things about yourself that you may not notice.
3. It's more fun.
4. Chances are you'll grow closer through the process and learn a lot about yourselves and each other.

Who might make a good partner?

A smart friend, a teacher, a mentor, an older sibling—basically anyone whose opinion you trust and whom you believe will hold you accountable.

Can I be a writing partner for someone who is my writing partner?

Of course! Supporting each other in this way is great.

How do I make sure that person holds me accountable?

Copy and paste the agreement on the next page into an email, or write your own version.

ACCOUNTABILITY AGREEMENT

Dear [enter name here]:

I'm going through a personal statement writing process, and I'm writing to ask if you'd be my accountability partner.

Why am I choosing you?

- Because you are awesome.
- Because I need someone to provide an outside perspective on my writing, and I think you would be a good person to help me.
- Because [enter other reason] _____.

What does it mean to be accountability partners? It means that I am committing to the following:

- Completing each of the goals listed below on each of the days listed.
- Letting you know by email (or text) if for some reason I am going to miss a deadline.
- Working hard on my assignments and doing my very best.

It means that you are committing to the following:

- Meeting with me to complete each of the goals listed below on each of the days listed.
- Letting me know by email (or text) if for some reason you have to reschedule with me.
- Being kind with criticism and offering useful notes for improvement.

Goals and potential meeting dates:

1. Select a topic for main personal statement. [Enter potential date here.]

2. Create an outline. [Enter potential date here.]
3. Write a first draft. [Enter potential date here.]
4. Write a second draft. [Enter potential date here.]
5. Write a third draft. [Enter potential date here.]

Are you willing to agree? If so, type your name in the blank below and email it back to me:

I, _____[your name here]_____,
do hereby agree to serve as accountability partner for _____
_____[my name here]_____ according
to the terms listed above. I recognize that this is not a legally binding
agreement, but that if I fail to fulfill my duties, I will be leaving my
partner (that's me) hanging.
   Signed, _____.

21 DETAILS EXERCISE

Make a list of twenty-one details from your life—interesting facts that
describe some small, random part of who you are.
   Here are eleven of my twenty-one details:

1. We moved twenty times while I was growing up, and I attended
   thirteen schools.
2. My biggest pet peeve is when the waiter takes my food
   before I've finished.
3. I eat salad with my hands. And never with dressing.
4. The worst feeling in the world is the dentist's air suction
   tube sucking air over my teeth.
5. I love popping bubble wrap.
6. When I was young, I used to use my finger to wipe off
   the top layer of toothpaste that I shared with my sister so I
   wouldn't get her germs.

7. I've never, ever seriously contemplated suicide.

8. I find most people fascinating and can talk to just about anyone.

9. I've won several awards in my life, but I'm most proud of these two: finishing second in the elementary school spelling bee when I was nine and being named MVP of the middle school floor hockey all-star game when I was eleven.

10. The most painful thing I ever experienced was breaking my kneecap in the tenth grade during a basketball game. The physical pain wasn't the worst part, though: it was losing the rest of the season and watching my team go 0–18.

11. My three younger brothers and I have never, as far as I can remember, ever had a fight.

See how each is a little tiny glimpse into my world? It's impossible to capture all of who you are in twenty-five or even 650 words, but with a few carefully chosen details, a portrait begins to emerge. Think of these twenty-one details as a collage.

Once you've written your twenty-one details, look for themes. Is there anything that comes up again and again? That may be a good theme for an essay, and this list can be especially useful for a supplemental essay that asks you to write a letter to your future roommate.

EVERYTHING I WANT COLLEGES TO KNOW ABOUT ME LIST

This exercise is simple, but extremely useful, especially in the middle or near the end of the process.

STEP 1: MAKE A LIST OF ALL THE THINGS YOU WANT COLLEGES TO KNOW ABOUT YOU.

How? Either:

• In a bullet-point format (organized, easy to read)

- On a blank sheet of paper (with drawings; get creative)
- On a time line (map out the major events in your life)

Note: I don't recommend a stream-of-consciousness free-write because those tend to get a little messy. By "messy," I mean they tend to bring forth a lot of words, but not a lot of specific, bullet point-able qualities that will help you get into college.

And that's the point of this list—to provide your counselor (or yourself) with a solid list of qualities, values, and cool stuff that might be interesting to a college admissions officer.

The main reason that this list is a good idea: it generates a list of details and possible topics for your personal statement, supplements, activities list, and additional information section.

Tips for creating a great list:

- **Have fun**. This doesn't have to be a chore. You're basically making a list of everything that's awesome about who you are and what you've done, which can be pretty darn affirming.
- **Create the list with a parent or friend**. Say to him or her: "Hey, I'm trying to make a list of all the reasons why a college should love me as much as you do—can you help me?"
- **Back up general stuff with specific examples**. For instance, suppose you think, "I can motivate people!" or "I stick with things I'm passionate about!" Provide a specific example to support your claim—or, better yet, one example that supports both claims! (Like the fact that you helped raise debate membership from nineteen to ninety-six at your school over four years.)

STEP 2 (OPTIONAL): ASK SOMEONE FOR HELP.

Once you've created your list, it can be great to get an outside perspective, so consider sharing it with whoever is helping you with your applications (friend/parent/counselor) and ask that person, "Can you help me make sure that all this stuff makes it into my application?"

Could you do this once your application is almost finished?

Absolutely. In fact, this will provide a checklist for making sure all the important parts of you are represented somewhere in your application.

STEP 3: DECIDE WHERE THE INFORMATION SHOULD GO IN YOUR APPLICATION.

Some options include:

1. Main statement
2. Activities list
3. Additional information section
4. Extracurricular essay (required only for some schools)
5. Another supplemental essay (required only for some schools)

TIME LINE OF MY LIFE EXERCISE

Here's one more exercise I love. This can be especially useful for students who have faced challenges, but it can also be useful for any student seeking perspective on the events of his or her life.

Step 1: Take out a blank sheet of paper and draw a line down the middle.

Step 2: Chart the major events of your life on the time line: any moves from one location to another, any births and deaths in the family, and anything else that you feel has shaped or changed you.

> Tip: Make room on your time line for "Before I was born" (Example: my parents came to the United States) and also for "After college" (Example: I will invent a cure for cancer).

Step 3: Once you've created your life time line, tell your life story to someone while that person just listens.

Step 4: Ask that person to help you identify the different "phases" of your life.

- Example 1: Life in Texas, Life in California (private school), Life in California (public school).
- Example 2: Pre-Divorce, The Divorce, Post-Divorce.
- Or, if you've experienced challenges, it might be: Challenges, What I Did, and What I Learned. (Turn to page 80 for more on this.)

CREATE A TIME LINE (VARIATION)

Step 1: Draw a line down the middle of a blank sheet of paper and hand it to a partner or mentor.

Step 2: Rather than creating your own time line, speak your life story aloud to a partner or mentor and have that person chart your life events on the time line for you. This frees you up as you talk.

Step 3: Once you've finished, have your partner tell you your life story back to you while you listen.

I actually prefer this variation because it allows the rare opportunity to hear someone else tell you your life story. The retelling can be done in pairs or before a larger group.

Once you've created the time line, work with your partner to identify the beginning, middle, and end of your essay. If possible, you can use narrative structure by identifying:

Type A

- Status quo: How did things used to be?
- Inciting incident: The event that started it all. The moment things began to change.
- Raise the stakes: What happened to build suspense for you—and others?
- Moment of truth/Turning point: Was there a moment when you had to make a big choice? Or when things were in danger of going down a dark path, but then turned around?
- New status quo: How are things now? (and perhaps) How have these experiences shaped you for [insert chosen career here]?

Or simply:

Type C

- Challenges
- What I did
- What I learned

Turn to page 74 for more on this.

List of Real Student Essays Included in This Book*

Knife by Hye Jeong Yoon	C	144
Five Families by Jesper Kim	D	152
**Why Did the Chicken Cross the Road? by Jacqueline Kwon	D	162
**Rock, Paper, Scissors by Christian Lau	D	169
I Shot My Brother by Alex Park	C	173
Dying Bird by Hye Jeong Yoon	C	176
Breaking Up with Mom by Katya Forsyth	C	192
Barbie vs. Terrorism and the Patriarchy by Tess Joseph	D	207
Grandma's Kimchi by Dong Jin Oh	A	209
Mazes by Jamie Tucker-Foltz	B	211

*Almost none of these students titled their essays (the exception is "Barbie vs. Terrorism and the Patriarchy"); I gave them titles to make referring to them easier.

**These are supplemental essays, submitted in addition to the main personal statement, while the rest of the essays in the book are main personal statements.

Acknowledgments

I STARTED MAKING A LIST of all those who have contributed to this book, then felt like I was planning a wedding and started to get nervous about the people I'd forget to mention. So I stopped and wrote this instead.

Thank you to all the amazing friends, mentors, and colleagues who've contributed so much, both directly and indirectly, to this book. You know who you are.

And thank you, in particular, to the students who so generously allowed me to use their essays for this book; to my best friend, Ryan Maldonado, who has taught me so much about writing; and to my wife, Veronica, and my daughter, Zola, who are my favorites.

Index

About the Author

ETHAN SAWYER IS A NATIONALLY recognized college essay expert and a sought-after speaker. Each year he helps thousands of students and counselors through his webinars, workshops, articles, products, and books, and works privately with a small number of students.

Raised in Spain, Ecuador, and Colombia, Ethan has studied at seventeen different schools and has worked as a teacher, curriculum writer, voice actor, motivational speaker, community organizer, and truck driver. He is a certified Myers-Briggs™ specialist, and his type (ENFJ) will tell you that he will show up on time, that he'll be excited to meet you, and that, more than anything, he is committed to—and an expert in—helping you realize your potential.

A graduate of Northwestern University, Ethan holds an MFA from UC–Irvine and two counseling certificates. He lives in Los Angeles with his beautiful wife, Veronica, and their amazing daughter, Zola.

To arrange for Ethan to speak at your school, conference, or event, go to www.collegeessayguy.com.